Advance Praise for *Mosaic Heart*

"Donna Mazzitelli integrally weaves the aspects of healing, reflection, and resolve into her life's journey. We become witness to the honest array of emotions and challenges when dealing with illness. Beautifully written, *Mosaic Heart* opens a gateway for anyone to go deeper into their own truth and healing."

—Janet L. Diederichs
Healing and Teaching Arts Practitioner

"To connect with a reader through honest sharing of the true thoughts and raw feelings of facing cancer and then elevate that same reader to feel strength, hope, and inspiration seems impossible. But that is what Donna Mazzitelli has done in her memoir, *Mosaic Heart.* Each chapter presents a different aspect of her experience with cancer and is a story in itself. And yet, the chapters weave together to paint a full picture of her immensely meaningful experience.

"Donna shares with such openness her journey through cancer ... a journey that took her to the depths of despair and then elevated her to the joy of understanding ... and then back again several times. Although she intentionally embraced her cancer experience as a way of learning about herself and growing as a person, she does not hide the intense highs and lows of the journey from diagnosis through treatment. She writes with the rare authenticity of a deeply spiritual person, sharing with raw honesty both the pain and joy of her tumultuous journey.

"I don't know anyone who has not been touched by cancer, either directly or indirectly—this book is a gift to us all. After reading *Mosaic Heart,* you will never think about cancer the same way again."

—Heather Kirby, LCSW, Author of *Wild At Heart:*
Adolescents, Horses & Other Kindred Spirits
Lead therapist at Kirby Creative Clinical Solutions

"Donna's memoir of surviving cancer twice is touching, personal, and intimate. She brought me into her inner life so I could experience it with her. Her optimistic, creative approach to one of the hardest times in her life gave me a new appreciation for what and how to survive a cancer diagnosis. I highly recommend Donna's inspiring book, including anyone who has or had cancer and especially for the people who love them."

—Ariana Strozzi Mazzucchi, Founder of Equine Guided Education, Author of *Horse Sense for the Leader Within* and soon-to-be-released *The Water Calls: One Woman's Journey to Reclaim Her Dignity and Freedom*

"A courageous, tender, heartwarming memoir that shows us a diagnosis can be a new beginning of self-care and self-love. Donna Mazzitelli is a brilliant storyteller and gifts every reader inspiration and hope that what is broken can be rebuilt. *Mosaic Heart* illuminates a heroine's journey. I couldn't put this beautiful book down."

—Devon Combs, Equine Gestalt Coach and Leader of Unbridled Retreats®, UnbridledRetreats.com

"I am honored to bear witness to Donna's work of heart and soul. This beautiful piece of art is a brilliant gift to the world. Raw and real, brave and authentic, truth abounding, a Heroine's Journey par excellence! Donna's journey is a roadmap for those willing to live a life with courage and commitment to owning their brilliance and Essential Selves—especially as women, living in a world where it is dangerous to own our truth and we are taught to hide our true selves.

"Donna's words ring true and honest as she shares the most vulnerable parts of herself and her life torn apart by illness, yet she courageously models the steps taken to traverse the age-old path of transformation. She teaches us by example how to navigate the Heroine's Journey with grace and grit, giving us hope and a guide for the ages by sharing her death and rebirth experience and the pathway to healing ourselves and the world through Love!"

—Lizanne Corbit, Author of *The Night Star* and *Notorious*, LizanneCorbitCounseling.com and SoulSpeaks.biz

"Donna Mazzitelli has a family lineage of cancer, fear, and unworthiness. *Mosaic Heart* is a journey of self-discovery, forcing Donna to face her darkest fears and rise above her ancestors' patterns of disease and unworthiness. Mazzitelli bravely sets out to heal and get to the heart of her cancer. She serendipitously learns that cancer has a silver lining, demonstrating she is not her DNA. She is worthy of love, and everything begins and ends with the Self, the I AM. Cancer isn't sexy. *Mosaic Heart* is raw, authentic, and inspirational."
—Alex Marcoux, Author of *Destination New Earth* and
Lifesigns: Tapping the Power of Synchronicity, Serendipity, and Miracles

"I loved this book! *Mosaic Heart* is personal, genuine, and engaging. Donna's mastery of the written word and enticing storytelling is breathtaking. It's such a cool experience going so deep with someone you know and getting a backstage pass to their inner workings. I'm a huge fan already—Donna is a true artist!"
—Ron Ben-Joseph. Content Creation, Storytelling,
and Performance Coach, ArtfulSpeaking.com

"*Mosaic Heart* helps us peer not only into Donna's life, but into our own hearts and life journeys. The vignettes, or pieces, weave together into a heartwarming story of courageous resilience, harnessed intuition, and tremendous strength that helped me discover more about myself as the reader. Curl up and dive into this incredible memoir told by a truly remarkable, loving, caring woman."
—Meghann Conter, Founder, TheDames.co global community
for high-caliber women leaders in business

"Donna is an amazing storyteller, weaving her past with her present to understand and accept her journey with breast cancer and beyond. Every woman's journey is a personal one, and Donna's will be an inspiration to so many. Her message that you need to accept and learn from the experience to be able to thrive and grow from it is powerful!"
—Michelle Hoglan, Visionary at The Boob Report
The Boob Report podcast on Spotify, iTunes,
Google Play, and TheBoobReport.com/podcast

"BRAVO!! Bold and brave. Raw and real. Donna Mazzitelli's memoir drew me in from the first page until the last, with intimate stories of her journey that I have no doubt will resonate with everyday life for each and every reader. Whether navigating ups and downs of health, relationships, or one's interior landscape, I believe *Mosaic Heart* will sound the call to many to BE ALIVE ... BE FREE ... and BE WHOLE."

—Sarah Davison-Tracy, Author of *Live Ablaze: And Light Up the World and No Longer Untouchable: A Story of Human Trafficking, Heroism, and Hope*, Speaker, Founder of SeedsOfExchange.org and RootedAndBeloved.org

"Donna Mazzitelli writes her memoir with vulnerability and grace. Often cancer treatment is hidden from others. I was gifted with understanding and compassion of the difficult process of cancer treatment and recovery by the author's courageous sharing of her journey. Thank you Donna for opening this chapter of your life to me!"

—Lisa J. Shultz, author of *Lighter Living* and *A Chance to Say Goodbye: Reflections on Losing a Parent*

"Donna Mazzitelli's memoir *Mosaic Heart* is about how facing cancer transformed her life.

"Wandering fabled streets and visiting ancient churches, she explored pieces of the mosaic of her life—including her lapsed Catholic faith and her once-strong connection with Mary, the mother of Jesus.

"The narrative's tension rises as the additional reasons behind Mazzitelli's stress are revealed: ... memories of relatives who suffered and died from cancer; ... accounts of her own struggle with the disease; ... concern over her troubled family relationships. The book is sensitive in describing emotions like grief, fear, and anger, which arose when Mazzitelli dealt with such issues. And its accounts of her solo forays in Florence, bolstered by the sense that Mary was bringing her hope, are a counterbalance and a source of release. Moving between Mazzitelli expressing resistance to self expression and yielding to her sense of self, the book's emotions are palpable.

"Through its focus on her inner world, the text reveals how Mazzitelli's inability to speak her innermost thoughts aloud left her feeling alone and voiceless. Examples of life events that made her hide her thoughts and feelings from others are given, contributing to the raw and troubling question of whether her inability to express her inner truth led to ill health. But the book also recouches illness as a wake-up call, and suggests that inner turmoil is a given when one is making profound personal changes."

Foreword Clarion Reviews
Clarion Review ★ ★ ★ ★

Mosaic
Heart

Mosaic Heart

Pieces of an Unfinished Life

DONNA MAZZITELLI

Merry Dissonance Press   Castle rock, Colorado

Mosaic Heart:
Pieces of an Unfinished Life

Published by Merry Dissonance Press
Castle Rock, CO

FIRST EDITION 2022

Publisher's Cataloging-in-Publication data

Names: Mazzitelli, Donna, author.
Title: Mosaic heart : pieces of an unfinished life / Donna Mazzitelli.
Description: Castle Rock, CO: Merry Dissonance Press, 2022.
Identifiers: ISBN: 978-1-939919-66-3
Subjects: LCSH Mazzitelli, Donna. | Life change events. | Cancer patients--Biography. | Breast--Cancer--Patients--United States--Biography. | Authors, American--21st century--Biography. | Self-realization (Psychology). | Healing. | BISAC BIOGRAPHY & AUTOBIOGRAPHY / Personal Memoirs | BIOGRAPHY & AUTOBIOGRAPHY / Women
Classification: LCC RC280.B8 .M39 2022 | DDC 616.99/449/092--dc23

ISBN 978-1-939919-66-3

Book Interior and Cover Design ©2022
Cover Art & Design by Melissa McQueen, CreativeReflections.Design
Interior Art & Design by Melissa McQueen, CreativeReflections.Design
Editing by Bobby Haas

Dedication

To my Nonna, Ada Rossi Casella;
to my father, Robert Harry Berridge;
and to my mother, Lida Jenny Casella Berridge;
who all walked pieces of a similar journey
through the landscape of cancer.
I know because of you that I have been given the opportunity
to thrive in life beyond cancer.

Panther came to me on the eve of
December's dark moon.
"My season has come," she said. "Winter is upon us.
Your season has come too. Listen!" she commanded.
"It's time to awaken the fire within.
Trust your inner knowing.
Reclaim your true power.
The most important relationship is with you.
Feel your light within the darkness.
Follow the signs.
Hush!
You are not alone.
I am with you always."

Prelude

Mosaics

"You realize you need to create a mosaic, don't you? Actually, two of them—the first for your broken heart and the second representing your rebuilt one. You've got to find the ceramic bowls, plates, and tiles to use and ask them how they want to be broken and what stories the pieces represent. I see a key too—an old-fashioned skeleton type. Yes, there is a key, and it will find you."

That's what a writing friend said to me after I read to her my first vignette. *What? What is she talking about?* I wondered. *I don't need to create a mosaic, let alone two. My book is called* Mosaic Heart *because of the pieces of my life. Why would I make an actual mosaic? If I decide my cover needs a mosaic image, I'm sure I can find a stock photo—or I can ask my girlfriend in California, a mosaic artist, to make one for me. I don't even know how to do mosaic work! And why would I take the time to create a mosaic, or two, when I need to be writing? I want an accountability partner to keep me on schedule, to keep me on track—not to create more diversions!* All of this ran through my head in a matter of seconds, yet I didn't speak a word of what I was thinking. I let our first meeting come to an end without another reference to mosaics.

Over the next few weeks, my resistance grew. By the time we had our second meeting, I announced, "I've decided I won't be creating a mosaic. While I'm in Florence, I'm certain I'll find the perfect centuries-old mosaics. I'll take pictures, and those photos might turn into my cover. But I'm not going to create a physical mosaic. I just need to write. I don't have time to make a mosaic, let alone two. I really don't. I've got so much work right now that I can hardly find time to write as it is."

"You're really resisting this, aren't you? Do you have any idea why?"

"I'm not resisting … I just don't think it's necessary, that's all. I already have part of my book written, and I don't see what purpose this will serve."

"I invite you to take a look at why you're resisting this so much. Because of your resistance, I really think there's something here."

I was furious. *How dare she keep persisting and insisting! How dare she "invite" me to take a look at why I don't want to do this! There's no reason to do it—that's why! It serves no purpose. What the hell! I am not a mosaic artist—I am a writer. What is her deal? This is about accountability, not art therapy!*

Once again, I said nothing out loud. Internally, I was fuming … and thankful I'd be leaving for Florence in a few days. It would give me a much-needed rest from my work life and a time to celebrate my recent recovery. It would also take me to the region where my maternal grandparents came from. I was going home to the land of my roots. Italy has always drawn me in. For as long as I can remember, the Mother Land has called to me. I'd been to Florence once before for a short visit, and I was excited to return to the ancient city I'd fallen in love with.

I got into my car and headed for home, glad to be putting distance between mosaics and me. Then it hit. Suddenly I saw in my mind's eye the pieces I'd work with. I saw one mosaic being made into another. I saw myself holding a jagged piece in my hands as I considered where it needed to go. As I touched the unfinished mosaic, tears welled up in my eyes. I tried to clear them so I could keep driving. *Damn it! Maybe I do need to make these … at least one of them.* As I sensed their significance, without seeing either mosaic clearly, I began to cry.

And without knowing exactly why, the tears continued to fall. *Somehow this is all part of my healing, isn't it? If I'm going to tell the stories I'm supposed to tell, that I* need *to tell, maybe I actually have to create these mosaics.* Taking deep breaths, I tried to calm myself. *You don't have to figure it out right now, so just try to relax.*

I couldn't explain why I'd gotten so emotional, but I sensed that all of this was part of tending to myself, of tending to my heart. I wasn't sure how I would do it or whether the mosaics needed to exist beyond metaphor, but I did know that the idea of mosaic pieces was integral to my writing. And somehow, my trip to Italy would help me begin to figure that out.

La Chiave (The Key)
Part I

At the airport in Florence, my friend Rosalie was waiting for me. She'd invited me to join her on this trip so we could catch up (it had been a year since we'd last seen each other) and for me to have an opportunity to do some reflective writing following my recent illness. I'd have a couple of days to myself while she did her two-day training session in the middle of our trip, and then we would take another two days to play together.

For the first day and a half, we exchanged stories as we took in the sites via the city's "Hop On Hop Off" bus touring system. Traveling around the center of Florence, we got a sense of the city's layout, which would make my days on my own easier to navigate. We found intimate, out-of-the-way places to eat, where we sat and talked nonstop about our personal lives in between mouthfuls of Florentine pizza, pasta, and salad.

The previous year when she'd visited me in Colorado, I had been living alone, separated from my husband for over a year. As we sat at my kitchen table, she made a statement that would turn out to be prophetic: "I see you and Dominic living here again together. You belong with each other, and this home is meant for the two of you." Now seated at an outside café, sipping cappuccinos and eating croissants in the early morning, I shared with her how, only one month after her visit, he had returned from Greece and began staying at the house. That temporary stay turned into our ultimate reunion a few months later. Rosalie and I continued to talk about all that had transpired in both of our lives, acknowledging the miracles we'd each experienced in a matter of months.

Eventually, we turned to the topic of writing. In the midst of sightseeing, we talked about our progress. As a fellow writer who remained unpublished, she shared what had been happening when she attempted to sit down and get serious. I told her about my most recent attempts, starts, and stops, along with the latest update on my "mosaic" story that now included a key as well as living, breathing mosaics. Rosalie and I had read some of our writing to each other the previous fall and had intended to encourage one another forward. Of course, life had gotten in the way for both of us. This trip was meant for us to reconnect and recommit to our craft.

On my first day wandering the streets alone, I made my way from the bus stop toward the Arno and came upon a Bombay chest in a storefront window. It was an antique piece with a skeleton key sticking out of the keyhole in the upper drawer. I was immediately reminded of the key that would find me, and I was convinced it was here in Florence. *Is this the one?* I laughed to myself, realizing it couldn't be since it was attached to a beautiful, and obviously very expensive, ornate wooden chest. The shop was most definitely upscale, and the antiques I could see through the window seemed elegant and well-preserved. Somehow, though, I sensed that this store was connected to my search. The shop was closed, so I made a mental note to stop in on my way back to the bus station. *Maybe they will have extra skeleton keys lying around.* I kept wondering, though, if this would be the way I'd find my key. After all, hadn't my friend told me, "The key will find you"?

On my way back to the *Firenze Santa Maria Novella* station, I stopped at the antique shop again. It was still closed. *Oh well,* I thought, *I guess I'll need to stay in the city center later tomorrow or start out earlier to catch them when they're open.* I couldn't hang out longer because I'd promised Rosalie that I'd get back by the time she finished her workday so we could make plans for the night.

That evening, I agreed to join her and her co-trainer, an Italian man named Stefano who I'd met the previous evening over dinner, for a group meal with their trainees at a restaurant back in the center of Florence. The trainees were from different parts of the world, and about half of the class had decided to participate in the night out.

The maître d' escorted us to the outdoor courtyard area, where bottles of *vino* and *aqua frizzante* awaited us on a long table that had been made ready for our group. Hours later, stuffed from our multicourse meal that included various local delicacies—*pane toscano* (saltless bread), *affettati misti* (meat and cheese platters), *tagliatelle funghi porcini e tartufo* (pasta with truffle and porcini mushrooms), and platters of prepared meats and vegetables—we ended with *cannoli* and plates of assorted Florentine cookies. I vowed to walk off our culinary excess the following day.

Back in *il centro*, I walked by the antique store once more and found that it was still closed. Wanting to take in as many historical structures as possible, I spent the day focused on churches and chapels and stopped for "selfies" along the Arno. As the day progressed, so did my awe-inspiring discovery of the many expressions of *La Madonna*. Unexpectedly, I began to connect with their *Madonna energy* in a way I'd never before experienced.

As a little girl who attended Catholic catechism classes, I loved "The Blessed Virgin Mary," the title most frequently used to describe Jesus's mother. For exemplary behavior in my fourth-grade catechism class, I'd been awarded a white plastic statue of Mary, and I cherished that figurine. Knowing that Mother Mary loved me with undying love, just as she loved her son, Jesus, was especially comforting whenever I felt misunderstood by my parents. I placed her on my childhood dresser to remind me that she was always there. She even came with me when I moved out of my childhood home. Years later, that statue disappeared, and I left the memory of her behind, along with my Catholic faith. Yet, here she was again, showing me that she'd never left my side. Just as I'd recently begun to rediscover angels and archangels in my life, Mary seemed to be telling me that I could also have a relationship with her.

When I entered the *Basilica di Santa Maria Novella* and walked along the walls to explore the crypts, paintings, and sculptures, I ended at a statue of Mary located at one of the side entrances. I found myself crying as I gazed upon her, somehow knowing that she was here to help me heal. The depth of her healing energy that enwrapped and infused my body was profound, and I couldn't seem to break away from her. I remained standing in front of the "Blessed Mother" for quite some time before I was ready to move on.

As I made my way to other churches, I began to focus more intently on the various expressions of Mary. Of the many that exist throughout Florence, the next one to bring me to tears was the Mary I encountered in Orsanmichele Church. The central feature of the building is the ornate tabernacle framing an exquisite painting by Bernardo Daddi of the "Madonna and Child with Angels" that replaced the original "painting of miracles" painted by a different artist and partially burned in a church fire. Mary—draped in her deep-midnight-blue mantle with a red under-fabric and red undergarment, seated on a red-and-gold patterned throne, holding the Child, and surrounded by inlaid gold angels—drew me forward. It wasn't solely the vibrancy of color—an energy seemed to beckon me to her. It was as if I could hear her telling me, "I am here to heal your family. Come forward and let me help." Her magnetic pull was penetrating, and I couldn't turn away.

In her, I found support for my two daughters, who were both struggling with intense young adult angst. Mary of Orsanmichele, as I came to call her, had a power I could not deny. I felt her love and compassion, her open heart and awaiting arms. Mary of Orsanmichele communicated to me through the chills that ran up and down my arms, legs, and torso that she was here to support my daughters in their struggles to seek independence and find themselves. She was also here to support Dominic and me as we continued to rebuild our relationship. I found myself sitting in the first wooden pew closest to the tabernacle so I could be as near to her as possible.

For decades, I had been completely disconnected from the faith of my heritage and upbringing, and I had no intention of returning to it, yet Mary of Orsanmichele spoke to me of motherly love, unconditional love, and her commitment to me and my family. "You have always been supported, dear child. And your daughters will always be supported too. Your family is held in my arms as I once held my son. I will never leave." The relief I felt at hearing those messages brought a cascade of tears. It was as if I'd been holding my breath through the challenges Dominic and I had endured over the past couple of years, and I could finally exhale. It was up to me to remember that I am not alone and I don't have to manage our family's challenges by myself; Mary was doing her best to remind me of that message.

After some time, I got up and lit candles, one for each of us, and then sat in her presence again as tears continued to stream down my cheeks. The power and authority of her tender presence were undeniable, and I was in no hurry to leave.

La Chiave (The Key)
Part 2

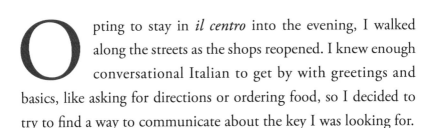

Opting to stay in *il centro* into the evening, I walked along the streets as the shops reopened. I knew enough conversational Italian to get by with greetings and basics, like asking for directions or ordering food, so I decided to try to find a way to communicate about the key I was looking for.

At the first shop I approached that had many old items on display, I entered and greeted the shopkeeper. *"Buongiorno!"* I said with a smile but then immediately realized that not only did I *not know* the word for key, but I couldn't find a similar word to get my message across. Opting for hand gestures to describe a skeleton key, I started by outlining with my fingers the circle at the end, followed by a long segment, and ended with downward strokes to indicate the teeth inserted into the lock. The shopkeeper exclaimed, *"Ah! Chiave!"* A smile appeared on her face, and I responded in kind, grateful that she understood my sign language. With the shaking of her head and a sad look replacing her smile, she communicated that, unfortunately, she didn't have such a key, nor did she know who might.

I then made my way to the antique shop that had first caught my attention. *"Buongiorno,"* I offered to the two ladies who greeted me at the door. *"Parla inglese?"* I asked.

"No," one of them responded with an apologetic look on her face. I decided to try and find a way to ask the question in Italian. However, as quickly as I'd learned the word for key, it was gone. So, once more, I gestured to let them know what I was seeking.

"Ah, chiave!" they exclaimed in unison. Unfortunately, they didn't have any keys that weren't attached to furniture. Using hand motions, I asked if they could suggest another place for me to visit, and they shook their heads that they could not. As I exited the shop, however, I spotted a storefront across the street that I'd not noticed during my previous excursions. The window display spoke of used furniture and secondhand items.

Once I entered, though, I started to wonder what kind of store it really was. To get to the heart of the store, I had to walk through a narrow passageway lined with furniture and "collectibles" on either side. The shop seemed more like a junk store, filled with clutter and mismatched items crammed together and piled in haphazard ways, each on top of the other. Not believing I'd ever find a key among so much chaos, I was just about to turn around and walk out when I noticed him. There, sitting in a chair, was the shop owner, an elderly man with gray hair, a stout yet sturdy build, and a pleasant, inviting face. We greeted each other, and because

I didn't want to appear impolite, especially since I was sure he'd noticed that I was searching for something, I once more used hand gestures to indicate what I was looking for.

"*Chiave,*" he spoke softly with a knowing smile. He pointed to my right, toward the floor. There, on the lower shelf of a sofa table, was a large round plate filled with skeleton keys. To its left, a small wooden chest contained more skeleton keys. How bizarre was this! I'd come looking for one key, and now I was faced with dozens of keys in a store that I initially thought I shouldn't have entered. With the realization that I had indeed found a treasure trove, I felt excitement building within me. *Calm down,* I told myself, as I took a deep breath and tried not to appear overly exuberant. I wanted to match his composed behavior, yet I felt trepidation. Something almost magical emanated from him, as if I'd entered another world and he'd appeared out of nowhere to make all my wishes come true.

My next thought was, *Oh shit! How will I ever choose?*

The shopkeeper got up and walked over to the plate. Picking it up, he crossed behind me to his desk, spread out a piece of white, silky fabric as if we were about to share a picnic lunch together, and gestured for me to begin my hunt. I picked up the "treasure chest" and placed it next to the platter he'd set down, feeling the intense heaviness of my need to make the right decision while I attempted to listen within for answers.

As I began my search, I once again wondered how the key would ever find me. With so many to pick from, I began by selecting those that were the shiniest—of varying sizes and with a variety of teeth patterns. The shopkeeper saw that I needed more room to spread them out, so he smiled at me and placed another cloth on the desk. It was clear that he wanted me to understand I could take as much time and space as was necessary to accomplish my mission. He was in no hurry. Soon, I had about twenty keys in front of me. How would I ever narrow down my search to just one? In a few more minutes, I had eliminated about half. I would just have to decide once I got home which was "the one."

"Quanto costa?" I asked.

"Dieci euro," he replied.

Wow, ten euro! Since the price seemed reasonable, I added one more to the pile from those I'd eliminated and asked again for the total cost. It was still ten euro.

"Si!" I replied.

As he began to gather the keys, he suddenly looked to the chest and grabbed another key, one that had never been a contender. With a smile and a nod, he added it to my find. He carefully wrapped the keys in white butcher paper and then selected just the right blue-and-white plastic bag that would be sturdy enough to hold them. We smiled at each other as we exchanged money and my purchase.

"Grazie mille!" I exclaimed. *"Ciao!"*

Exiting the shop, I realized what had just happened. My key had indeed found me. *La chiave* that he had chosen for me was coming home to Colorado. The most interesting aspect of the key: it was tarnished and rusty looking—not at all what I'd been drawn to as I sorted through the piles. This key was neither the largest nor the smallest, and its teeth were rather common. *Nothing special, nothing grandiose,* I thought as I made my way to the bus station.

On the ride back to the hotel, I considered what had just happened. Isn't it oftentimes the simplest, most non-descript things that hold the biggest magic and the greatest meaning? I considered the shop, which I'd almost exited because it wasn't as upscale as the surrounding stores. And then there was the shop-keeper. His smile and his mannerisms had been unimposing and gentle, yet his kindness and generosity felt immense. I'm sure he had no idea just how important his gift was to me. Looking down at my bag, I was reminded how our life lessons are often offered to us through the most ordinary experiences. If we keep our eyes and ears and hearts open, those lessons can continue until we take our last breath. My lessons were most definitely far from over. As I once again felt chills up and down my body, I knew that, indeed, *this key* had much to teach me.

When I returned to our hotel that evening, I could hardly wait to tell Rosalie what had happened. She was out for a run, so I had a few minutes to calm down before she got back.

Soon enough, the door clicked, and Rosalie entered the room. "You won't believe what happened today!" I exclaimed.

"Well, I have something to tell you too," Rosalie replied, "but you go first."

I told her everything that had transpired that day and how my key had truly found me. "That's incredible," she said. With a huge smile on her face, she added, "Well, you're *really* not going to believe what I'm about to tell you. It's kind of crazy, actually."

Rosalie recounted how she'd been so full from the previous

night's dinner that she couldn't fathom eating the spread laid out for their group's lunch. "I decided to go for a walk-run instead. Somehow, I ended up in an area that was rural, with farmhouses and lots of open space. I came upon a building and noticed something lying on the ground that immediately made me think of you and your book. There, spread out, were pieces of broken tiles and clay pots, way more than I could ever carry. I decided it was about me bringing back to you a few special pieces rather than hordes of them. I also considered that you would only be able to bring back a small amount in your suitcase anyway, so I used my tissue to hold the pieces and picked ones that represented the various colors on the ground." Holding the folded tissue in her hand, she added, "So these are intended to get your mosaic started."

With that, she opened her tissue and spread the pieces on the bed in front of me. *Earth tones.* There were gold, yellow, green, and rust-colored pieces. One piece struck me most of all. It was striped and shaped like a keyhole. "The heart of my mosaic, the centerpiece," I said out loud as I picked it up. I immediately wanted to go back and gather more.

"I think these are supposed to be the beginning … a part of what you'll include," Rosalie said. "I don't believe you're supposed to take all the pieces you'll need from here."

"Yes, I guess you're right. *That* would be way too easy."

We both laughed.

Another element of divine intervention. Not to give me all the answers at once. Just enough to propel me forward. Enough to help me know I am on the right path. Just like life. Unfolding and revealing more. One more piece of information and validation to continue. Most importantly, the opportunity to take pieces of Italy, of my roots, back home with me.

More will be revealed, I thought. *Be patient, keep your eyes and ears open, and stay willing.* With willingness, grace always comes. Even by way of a key and broken pieces of tile.

Teacher, Friend, Ally

My trip to Florence became the jumping-off point to look more deeply at my experience with an illness that held the potential to end my life prematurely. Being in Florence also gave me the time and distance to consider the other recent coinciding life events, putting it all into the context of beginning to heal more deeply and live life more fully.

Illness has a way of offering a wake-up call. It reminds us that life has a beginning, middle, and end. It encourages us to consider how we are currently living. Are we embracing life or sitting on the sidelines? Are we fighting the current of life at every turn or joining its flow, embracing life's challenges, obstacles, and miracles? Are we living as a shadow walker, afraid to come into the light, or are we standing up and out in all our brilliance? Illness provides the invitation to take a serious look at how we want to live—and even *if* we want to live.

Cancer showed up in my fifties and began as an unexpected, imposing intruder—something to be feared and fought against. Something to be excised. Something to be eradicated. Ultimately, cancer turned out to be my closest friend and my most honest and life-affirming ally.

Less than a year after my trip to Florence with Rosalie, I returned to Italy with my sister and mother. Italy had become a place of solace and profound knowing that I am and always have been supported and held in immense love by all who came before me. The land of my ancestors continued to be the place of encouragement to reflect, to heal more deeply, and to write. My writing did not start in Italy, and it did not finish there, but it was tended to and nurtured through the people and experiences that encouraged me to tell my story.

Mosaic Heart represents my deep dive into the exploration of parts of my life, most especially my marriage, family life, and my life's purpose beyond midlife, as well as my journey with cancer. The stories are presented in the order that best reflects the opening of my awareness to a particular part of my life, not necessarily in chronological order, but how my deeper exploration unfolded. *Mosaic Heart* encompasses what I know at this point in time—how I've lived, how I've seen my life, what I've come to understand, and where I intend to go from here.

Mosaic Heart is not a book solely about cancer, but cancer is an integral part of this story. Without cancer having entered my life, I'm not sure I would be where I find myself today—learning more about self-love, self-compassion, and the ability to share that love and compassion outwardly with others. Have I arrived at the mountaintop of complete and constant love and compassion for myself and others? Do I love myself unconditionally today? Do I have compassion for myself twenty-four seven? Of course not! This is a journey, and it will continue for as long as I live and breathe. What I know today, though, is that I have more love and compassion now than I did in my twenties, thirties, forties, and even my fifties. I also know that to continue to be a teacher and a friend, cancer doesn't have to remain with me. I expect that as time goes on and more of life unfolds, my heart will continue to expand and grow, and this mosaic heart of mine will feel more and more integrated with each passing year.

I offer this collection of vignettes—these fragments and pieces—in love and with compassion for wherever you may be at this moment in your life. Blessings to you and your journey.

First
Movement

Cancer knocked at my door in January.
We became acquainted in February.
I asked her to leave in March.
She stayed until June.
I don't expect she'll pass this way again.

The Visit

G oing to doctors and even dentists has always made me nervous. A doctor visit usually meant additional pain, especially when I needed a shot.

I hated shots. They scared me, and they hurt. When it was time to get them at five years old, I hid against the back wall of the examination room, under the examining table. Far enough away that I thought I'd be safe. Far enough away that I thought no one would be able to reach me. I was not going to let them touch me or hurt me. For a fleeting moment, I thought I'd succeeded. But then arms began to grab at me underneath the table. I pushed myself harder against the wall, hoping I could outsmart them and get beyond their reach, maybe even disappearing into the wall. Ultimately, it didn't work.

It took a doctor, a nurse, and my father to pull me out from under the table. As they did, I kicked and screamed and squirmed, trying with all my might to break free. I wasn't going to allow them to poke me. Unfortunately, my fight quickly turned out to be all for nothing. With the doctor and my father holding me down as I screamed and shouted "No!" the nurse administered the shots.

My protests fell on deaf ears. The deed was done. I whimpered as the pain subsided. Then, I got quiet. It was over, and I'd lost. There had been nothing I could do to stop what I didn't want. Nothing.

As I grew older, I understood that there were instances when shots were necessary. My fear of them and the pain they caused lessened. In time, I learned to accept that they sometimes had to be administered to overcome an illness or to prevent one. I began to realize that visits to the doctor's office were necessary at times, too, especially because I suffered from earaches and often needed treatment and medication to alleviate the pain and prevent my eardrum from rupturing. But, no matter what, my fear and distrust of doctors never completely left me.

As an adult, I saw doctors as the ones looking for a problem. Not wanting them to discover a problem, yet sensing I was there to find one, maybe even more than one, I always approached appointments with apprehension. After all, isn't that what doctors do—seek out what is incongruent, what is out of place, and what has changed? Except for well-baby checks, the focus is on examining and testing to see if anything has popped up that needs to be addressed. Although I always told myself that I was there to receive a clean bill of health—to be pronounced healthy once more—deep down, I worried that *this time this doctor* would make a different pronouncement.

With each visit to a doctor, I tried to pretend I didn't carry this fear, but it was always just under the surface. And it usually bubbled up and out through my defiant behavior as I impatiently filled out forms, thinking, *Of course I'm checking "no" to every condition or disorder—I'm healthy, dammit!* At times, my responsive coldness came out as a nurse's aide showed me to my room and took my vitals. Sometimes, I resented when told to strip and put on the gown with the opening in the front. *I don't really need to be here,* I would tell myself. *I just do this to appease my family.* Occasionally, I was downright rude to the poor nurses' aides who were just doing their jobs to ensure they had gathered all the information the doctors would need.

On this particular day, January 23, my behavior was no different. To cover up my fear of seeing a new doctor in my new home state of Colorado, I was huffy and impatient. *How many forms does a person need to fill out before they can be seen? Don't they have my records from California?*

As in the past, I once again checked "no" for every known human condition—well, almost every one. The list seemed to get longer each time I returned to a doctor. How many disorders, diseases, and illnesses could there be? Apparently a lot! I did have to record two surgeries: one a tonsillectomy at five years of age and the other the C-section I had when my twin daughters were born.

I also had to admit to one "yes" on the form. Menopause. Yes, I was now officially a crone—I'd completed the transition during my fiftieth year of life. At fifty-one, I could no longer deny that I was aging. Although I didn't carry within my body the history of my family's medical conditions that included cancer and heart disease,

I finally had to check my first "yes" box, and I didn't like it one bit. It made me uncomfortable and agitated—and more fearful. *After checking this one box, won't it be downhill from here? And what else might they find wrong with me today?* I struggled to push down that question, swallowing it back like bile.

After my just-under-the-red-zone level of rudeness and impatience with the nurse's aide, I was left on my own. My vitals looked good—that was a good sign. *Maybe everything else will go smoothly too.* I chastised myself for my unkindness and impatience. These were not my normal modes of operation—at least not outside a medical or dental office. I was not usually rude or mean to anyone I encountered throughout my day. *I need to lighten up,* I thought. *No one deserves to be treated unkindly.*

I sat in the sterile room, my paper gown dutifully opened at the front, and I wrapped it tightly around myself. I kept my socks on my feet. After all, it was January in Colorado, and I knew soon enough I'd be placing those feet in the cold, metal stirrups. I attempted to look at a magazine to keep myself distracted while waiting to meet my new doctor.

Doing a mental check-in, I acknowledged just how nervous I was as I sat at the edge of the exam table. I didn't like doctor examinations under normal circumstances, and having to be examined by a *new doctor* made me extremely anxious and concerned. Would I like her as much as my doctor in California? Would I come to trust her? Would we make a connection? I hoped so. Scanning my body, mind, and heart, I also recognized how badly I felt about my behavior thus far. I admonished myself for my shortness with the aide. She hadn't done anything wrong, and I knew it. These were my issues. No one had forced me to be here. I'd made the appointment and chosen the doctor and the day. All of my own accord. That young woman hadn't deserved my snootiness.

I vowed to act polite and kind if she returned to my room. Grateful, too, because, after all, she had continued to be polite and acted as if I had been the easiest patient in the world to deal with. She'd responded to me as if I were treating her with the utmost respect. I hadn't been cruel or extremely difficult, just cold, brusque, and unsmiling. *If she returns, I will show her the real me and even humble myself and apologize for my earlier behavior.* I was determined to improve upon the impression I'd made thus far.

Suddenly, I heard a knock at the door, and in walked a young woman in her early thirties—blond hair, slender, and tall—reminding me that I was definitely getting older. She could have been my daughter! She smiled warmly and approached me with an outstretched hand. *This is my opportunity to start turning things around.* I returned a smile and put out my hand in greeting. When our hands joined, I knew I'd chosen the right doctor. Her caring and unrushed demeanor showed through. As I clasped her hand, a warm thought filled every part of me: *This female doctor is going to provide me with what I need most from her—a genuine connection.*

The Discovery

Some women find a lump as they shower, touching something they never felt before. Nonna, my Italian grandmother, found hers as she stood in front of her bathroom mirror while drying herself after a morning bath. At that moment, on that particular day, at sixty-two years of age, she could see and feel an obvious bump on her left breast that hadn't been noticeable days before. That bump turned out to be cancer that had already metastasized into her chest.

The treatment at the time was radical surgery and radiation, and she underwent both. She lived more than another decade until the cancer spread inside and outside her body. She lived long enough to see the first of her four grandchildren marry. Four months after that joyous event that she attended in a wheelchair, she died. Her funeral was on my sixteenth birthday. "Sweet sixteen and never been kissed," a relative said to me. *Sweet sixteen and experiencing death,* I thought. *My most favorite person has just died.*

Thirty-five years later, on January 23, 2007, my lump was discovered in a routine annual checkup as my new female physician palpated my right breast. I had not had a checkup in a little over a year, not since we'd moved from California to Colorado at the end of 2005. I'd made a New Year's commitment to myself to get one at the start of the year.

"Hmm. I'm feeling something that seems a bit unusual," she said as she continued to palpate my right breast.

"What?" I asked. "Is it a cyst?"

"It's probably nothing, but the shape and feel is different than a cyst. Here, you can feel it," she said as she placed my fingers on the area.

"Is it a plugged duct maybe? I felt it recently and thought that's what it was."

"No, I don't believe so. I'd like you to have it checked. I want you to get a mammogram and ultrasound. I'm sure it's nothing, but I want to be safe. Let's be safe. If they feel it's warranted, they'll do a biopsy at the same time," she explained.

I should have taken the cue from those words … mammogram … ultrasound … biopsy. There was more to this story, although her facial expressions gave away nothing.

I don't remember my pap smear or anything else that followed, other than standing by her office door after I got dressed and watching as she filled out the orders. I wanted to hear assurances—I needed to hear words that told me everything

45

would be fine and that this would all turn out okay. That whatever "this" was—whatever she'd felt—was *really nothing*. A cyst maybe or a plugged duct like I'd developed when I was nursing my twin daughters. The ones that caused mastitis. The ones that long ago led me to an oncological surgeon to be further investigated and then turned out to be nothing more than a bad infection. This had to be another *nothing*—it just had to be. Of course, I got no such assurances—just a piece of paper with written orders on it, a smile, and confirmation that the results would be sent to her.

The mammogram and ultrasound were done at the same appointment, but then the radiologist told me they wanted to do a biopsy. "Just to be safe. It's probably nothing—90 percent of these turn out to be nothing," he tried to assure me as I tried to read his and the tech's faces. I sensed that all wasn't *nothing* and that more was going on than the need *to be safe*, but I couldn't get verification from either of their faces or their body language. They were good at masking their true thoughts and feelings, I realized later.

At one point, I did detect concern from the tech—it was an underlying sympathetic look as if she were saying, "I'm so sorry this is happening, but we'll help you get through it." I couldn't tell if she was sorry I needed to go through these tests or if she knew it was cancer. Deep inside, I knew we were dancing around the word that began with a big "C," but no one would say it out loud. We all sidestepped and tried to move away from the thought of it. "Unfortunately, the schedule is full today, but we'll try to get you in as quickly as possible. It's going to be okay; you're going to be okay," she added.

How could she say that? Did she have a crystal ball? Did she know something I didn't?

"Do you think it's cancer?" There! I finally said the word that I was certain all of us were thinking anyway.

"We won't know anything until we do the biopsy, but as I've said, most of these turn out to be nothing. Usually just a false alarm. I'm sure yours will turn out to be nothing too," the radiologist said with a smile on his face.

There was that word again: *nothing*. When I looked over at the tech, she wasn't wearing a smile. She was straight-faced, and I sensed she was doing her best to keep her thoughts and emotions camouflaged. I think she already knew how this was going to go: nothing wouldn't turn out to be nothing at all. And a smile couldn't begin to reflect that journey.

Nonna

The week between the ultrasound-mammogram and the biopsy seemed like forever. It was difficult to focus on anything other than what might be going on. As much as I didn't want to talk about cancer, I couldn't help thinking about it. The first time cancer impacted my life was through my grandmother's life and death. During the week I waited to have the next test, I often thought about her. Nonna's lump had turned out to be anything but *nothing*, and the ultimate loss of her from my life had been devastating.

Nonna was one of my biggest teachers. She was also my biggest advocate. Without a doubt, I knew she loved me. When she was around or when we visited her, I felt lovable.

Nonna was quiet, but we understood she had her opinions. She also had her ways of working around whatever was happening.

When she sensed that her action might agitate my nonno, she did it discreetly so the action didn't stand out. Sometimes she worked around my mother too. It might have seemed sneaky or secretive, but it was her way of spoiling us just a little.

For instance, she often colluded with my sister, Debbie, and me to give us a treat we would enjoy, such as a piece of candy. She would instruct us not to tell our mother. It wasn't that the three of us were doing anything wrong—she just didn't want to deal with my mother's disapproval or attempts to stop her from showing us her love through her generosity. She didn't want my mother to ruin the pure enjoyment she experienced by giving us a treat that we didn't get every day. It was usually a food item or small gesture, like fifty cents to tuck away so we could buy our own candy or gum at the store, but to the two of us, it felt like the grandest of gestures.

Nonna was an extremely patient woman. Even when my nonno ranted, she kept her cool. I know it cost her internally, but outwardly, she never engaged in escalating his ire or feeding his anger. Usually, she dismissed it like a fleck of dust she wiped away with her cleaning rag.

Using that same patience, Nonna taught me how to knit, embroider, and crochet. She and I would sit for hours on our couch as she showed me these skills and let me practice. I still have some of the dish towels I embroidered while sitting at her side. We knitted slippers, which she called *ciabattas*, and created beautiful, embroidered scenes on our bleached white linens.

Debbie and I were thrilled when Nonna came to spend a week in our home each summer. Her visit meant homemade waffles in the morning and plenty of her gentle and lighthearted attention.

We knew how much she loved us through her actions. I especially loved the calm she brought with her. No matter what tension existed between my father and mother, which usually related to my dad's overconsumption of alcohol at a social event or after work with his buddies, Nonna's presence meant we would be fine. She always made me feel safe and secure.

Nonna did her best to teach Debbie and me Italian. As Nonna and I knitted or embroidered, she would teach me words and a few phrases. If she was disappointed about anything in her life, it was that we didn't learn to speak her Mother Tongue. She and my mom conversed in Italian, but because my dad only spoke English, my mom never tried to speak to us in Italian. Without reinforcement from my mom, we had no way to retain all the words and phrases Nonna tried to teach us. Although we never did learn to converse with her, Nonna never made us feel bad. She offered it as a gift from her to us—and no ridicule or accusation went with it.

Losing Nonna just before my sixteenth birthday was a big blow. I lost a guide, a calm presence, a teacher, and a friend. I lost the only living grandmother I'd ever known. I lost the relative who was the first to connect me with my roots in Italy, and the one who made me feel special. With her death, I also lost my sense of innocence. Good people, kind people, sweet people could get sick and die. It could happen to anyone at any time.

Within months of my grandmother's death, I was delivered another blow. The most important man in my life, my father, would be handed a death sentence in his late thirties. Yes, cancer could be the bearer of sickness and death, no matter one's gender or age.

My Father

While I was growing up, my father rarely took extra time off work, other than our annual summertime family vacation. I clearly remember three occasions when he did. One was for fun—he arranged to have a Saturday off so he could take his family to see snow over a two-day weekend. The other two occasions were due to illness. The first time he had to stay home for health reasons was also my first recollection of seeing my father in pain.

When he was a child, he had never gone to a dentist. He received his first dental care while in the army. By the time he saw an army dentist, it was already too late. A poor diet in childhood, along with a lack of dental care, left him with a mouthful of rotting, decaying, and dying teeth. Yet, even as bad as his teeth were, my father didn't want to lose them. For a number of years, dentists tried to do what they could to prevent their extraction. Eventually, it became clear, even to my father, that his teeth needed to come out.

Not yet old enough to attend kindergarten, I peered around the corner after my midday nap. "Don't disturb your father," my mother had instructed me earlier. "He's not feeling well right now." I needed to see for myself just how bad it was. My daddy was usually never home that early in the day.

I spied him sitting in a chair, staring out our front-room window, oblivious to what was going on around him. Sticking out of his mouth was pinky-red, blood-soaked gauze. I knew he wouldn't be able to speak to me, so I stayed back. I was extremely sad and frightened as I watched my daddy from around the corner. He sat very still and continued to gaze out the window. I had never before seen him so quiet and withdrawn. It scared me to see him bleeding, and I sensed that he was hurting badly. I wanted to go to him and sit in his lap like I often did, but I sensed he wouldn't want me to see him like that. I also knew he wouldn't be able to hold me in his arms. I stayed back and continued to watch him from a distance until my mom found me standing there and told me to go play in my bedroom.

No one ever explained to me what had just happened to my father. The man who usually wore a smile that went all the way to his gorgeous "Frank Sinatra" eyes, the man who scooped me up in his arms when he got home from work and sat me in his lap each day was nowhere in sight. Scared for my father, and for me, I did what I was told and went to my bedroom. Rather than play, though, all I could do was worry about what would happen next.

Over a decade later, and just months after my grandmother died, I came home from school and found out that my dad was in the hospital. He had been involved in an automobile accident while delivering bread for Wonder Bread, a well-known American company where he'd spent most of his adult working life.

In the emergency room, they discovered that his spleen had ruptured, and he underwent emergency surgery. In the course of removing my dad's spleen, the surgeon saw something suspicious and took a biopsy of his liver. It turned out to be cancer.

While still recovering in the hospital, the surgeon referred my father to an oncologist—after telling him that he believed he had less than a year to live. With tears streaming down the sides of his face as he lay in his hospital bed, my father told us what the surgeon had said. Wanting to be strong for my dad, I left his hospital room and stepped into the hallway, where I cried as quietly as possible. I couldn't lose my dad as well as my grandmother. At that moment, I hated cancer with all my being. It robbed families. Cancer had taken my grandmother and now was determined to take my dad as well. Being a junior in high school, I didn't know how I'd survive it.

Once my father was released from the hospital and saw the oncologist, everything changed. After his oncologist reviewed the biopsy results and conducted more tests, the cancer was given a name: non-Hodgkin's lymphoma. His prognosis went from months of life to an indefinite amount of time—my father could live with this disease for years. Exactly how many, no one could say. His oncologist explained that he would not need to undergo any treatment until the time came when the cancer became "active." His doctor believed that undergoing treatment prematurely would render it ineffective when my father would really need it—and his doctor did believe that one day he would. He explained that they would start with monitoring his condition: bloodwork and lymph node measurements every three months.

Three-month checkups turned into six-month checkups and eventually turned into checkups once a year, which stretched out for more than two decades as the cancer remained in remission. What might have happened had the cancer not been discovered, no one knows. Our family chose to believe that his auto accident saved my father's life.

The Biopsy

The day I returned for my biopsy, I had a different tech. She explained that we would do an ultrasound first to mark the spot where the biopsy would be performed. As she showed me the area on the ultrasound, I probed her gently to see if she would give me any straight answers to my questions. Did they think I had cancer? Was that why they wanted to do the biopsy? I did my best to ask in an indirect way.

"So, as you look at that area, what does it seem like? What does it look like to you?" I obviously hadn't been so indirect after all.

"Well, this is the area that is suspicious—this is the area that seems to be malignant," she replied.

She'd said it. She'd actually said it! She had given me more than I'd expected—a straight answer with a definitive word: malignant.

"So, this is what cancer looks like … this looks like cancer?"

"Yes," she answered. "This is the area they'll be extracting from."

I tried to pretend that nothing alarming had just been said. I tried to act as if I'd known all along that it was cancer—that they'd already disclosed their suspicions to me. Inside I began to crumble. From that moment on, I shut down. Except for the pain of the biopsy—which was more psychic than physical—and the noise the "sucking machine" made as it gathered an indiscriminate sampling of cells from my breast, I tried not to think about what was happening or where this would all lead.

The radiologist and second technician simultaneously smiled at me as the radiologist held the tubular wand that was extracting my breast tissue. At that moment, I winced.

"Are you in pain?" the radiologist asked.

"Not really. I just *feel* the horrible sound as this machine is sucking out tissue." Almost directly in front of my face, I watched my breast tissue being sucked up and into the long, clear plastic tube. "I feel the horror of having my tissue vacuumed up."

He looked at me quizzically but only replied, "It won't be much longer."

When he pulled out the probe, I began to bleed—apparently more than expected. They got another person to help, and the two techs pushed down hard on my breast. They seemed alarmed at how much I was bleeding. I tried to calm down. By now, however, I was scared. And their faces, filled with concern, only made me feel more afraid. All I could think about was how my body, which had always supported me, was now betraying me. *Cancer and excessive bleeding—will I survive this? Any of this? Could this be the end of my life? Why now?* I felt as if I'd only just begun to live.

I might have been fifty-one years old, but I still had two eleven-year-old daughters to raise and a black belt to achieve side by side with them. I was halfway there. And I still hadn't figured out what I wanted to be when I grew up. *This can't be how my life ends, can it? From breast cancer? Now?* Tears rolled down the sides of my face as I lay immobile and scared while they continued to push down on my chest.

"We are not going to do the other spot today. We don't want to risk more bleeding. When you come back for the sentinel node biopsy … if that becomes necessary," he added almost as an afterthought, "we'll get the other place then."

Overwhelm and shock washed over me. *Sentinel node biopsy? If that becomes necessary?* I didn't dare ask him to explain—I couldn't deal with anything more at that moment. I just wanted to go home. I wanted to put all of this behind me for now. I wanted to forget, at least until they called with the results.

As Dominic and I headed for home, I told him what the tech had said. I was sure it was cancer. She'd pretty much confirmed it during the ultrasound. She'd explained that an area looks a certain way when the mass is cancer, as opposed to how it looks when it is a benign cyst or growth. The area in me looked the way it does when it is cancer.

Once again, I went into waiting mode. Just like the week between my scheduled mammogram and biopsy, I had to wait another week for results.

During that week, I thought more about those who'd come before me and had cancer: Nonna and my father, who were now both deceased. Even my mother had undergone a lumpectomy the previous year at the age of seventy-six. Post-menopausal breast cancer and non-Hodgkin's lymphoma. Maybe it was the Law of Attraction at work, but I'd always feared and secretly believed I'd have cancer one day. I just hadn't expected it at this point in my life. I thought I'd be much older—at least in my sixties. I thought it'd be much later in life—after my daughters were grown up.

In the days before the call came from the radiologist, I thought back to the women in my life, those who'd had cancer and those who hadn't. My nonna and my mother had both been diagnosed with post-menopausal cancer, yet my aunt, who was five years older than my mom, had never had cancer. Neither had my sister. My grandmother had three sisters in Italy, and one of them had died from breast cancer. So, it seemed I had a fifty-fifty chance. *Which group will I ultimately land in? Which club will I join? What will my membership look like, and what will be the price of admission?*

As the week progressed and I got further away from the biopsy, another thought struck me. I realized that my body hadn't betrayed me. It had actually given me a gift. Because of the excessive bleeding at the time of my procedure, I hadn't been subjected to further biopsy or had to experience further trauma physically, emotionally, and psychically. My body had taken care of me that day. It had gifted me with a reprieve. And no matter what happened next, I had to trust that it would take care of me in the future too.

The Call

The caller ID reflected the number I'd been watching for, the call I'd been waiting for, the call I'd been dreading. I decided to take it in the privacy of my bedroom sitting area, away from our adolescent daughters. Dominic stood by my side, watching for my reaction to the caller.

"Mrs. Mazzitelli?" the radiologist began. "Is this Mrs. Mazzitelli?"

"Yes, this is she."

"This is Dr. R. I'm calling with the results of your biopsy. I'm afraid I have some not-so-good news."

My breath caught in my throat. I wasn't aware of anything except the sound of his voice.

"The biopsy revealed that it is cancer. But ... if you're going to get cancer, you got the best one. It is Grade 1, the least aggressive."

Is he serious? Does he really think I'll hear this as good news? Is he trying to keep the conversation light so I won't start to cry? I couldn't do that anyway. Not until I was off the phone. Not until I was completely alone. And even then, would I be able to cry? Or would I be too numb, too closed off and sealed up to unleash all that I kept locked inside? Just as I'd done as a child, and in my more recent attempts to be a supportive wife, I didn't usually allow myself the time or space to cry or even to acknowledge that I was having an emotional reaction and needed to tend to what I was feeling and thinking. *Is now any different?*

His voice brought me back to the present. "The next thing you need to do is schedule a sentinel node biopsy. That way, we can determine the stage, you know, to see if it has spread to other places. The area involved seems to be small, about one centimeter, but we do need to determine if it's localized."

"Do I really need to do a sentinel node biopsy? I don't want to cause the cancer to spread by messing with my lymph nodes. I remember the doctor telling my father that they wouldn't go in surgically until absolutely necessary because they didn't want his lymphoma to spread. They didn't want to give the cancer oxygen. I don't want to do that either."

"Your father had lymphoma, a completely different type of cancer. I'm sure it had more to do with it being lymphoma than any other reason. Mrs. Mazzitelli, there is nothing to be concerned about. Sentinel node biopsies are done all the time to determine the stage of cancer prior to developing a treatment plan," he replied.

Dominic was standing next to me and whispered, "Ask him what he'd do if it were his wife."

"If you were my wife, I'd have you get the sentinel node biopsy right away and schedule surgery as soon as possible. I've never heard about the concern you expressed. I'd just get it done as quickly as possible."

"Okay," I responded automatically.

"So, call the surgery center and make that appointment."

I got off the phone and stared out at nothing in particular. *Cancer. I've got cancer. How can this be? I eat healthy. I exercise. We eat organic food. I don't drink or smoke ... haven't in decades. How did I get this? How?*

Just as I thought would happen, I didn't cry. I was too shocked, too numb, too incredibly overwhelmed. All I could think was *cancer ... cancer ... cancer ...*

"We'll take care of this. We'll deal with this and get rid of it. We'll get through this together. Whatever we have to face, we'll face it together. Whatever's going to happen, whatever has to be done, we'll handle it and get past this," Dominic said, his words as much for himself as for me. "We'll get it cut out as quickly as possible. Whatever you have to do to get rid of it, we'll do. We'll get past this."

Take care of it? Deal with it? Get through it? Get past it? Handle it? But what is IT? What will we handle? What will we face and deal with together? A lumpectomy? A mastectomy? Chemo? Radiation? Dying? I have two daughters to raise! I can't die!

The thoughts in my head ran at lightning speed. I wanted to scream. Instead, I stayed quiet and didn't express anything. Not my anger. Not my sense of betrayal. Not my indignation. Not my shock. Not my fear. Not my immense sadness.

61

Dominic took me in his arms. "We'll get through this, Donna. You're going to be okay. *You are!*" he pronounced.

I pulled away because I couldn't stay in his arms. I wasn't ready to feel anything—not love, not support, not assurances, not sympathy, and most especially, not fear. I wasn't ready to open up and be vulnerable.

There was no *we* in that moment. Only a *me* who had no idea what to do next.

Valentine's Day ...
Take 1

"It's cancer," were the words I received from a man I'd only seen once. On Valentine's Day, the day of love, romance, candy, flowers, cards, candlelight dinners, and lovers, the day when people profess their undying love and devotion to each other, I received the pronouncement of my fate—"You have cancer." I sat there wondering how I'd get through the next twenty-four hours. *How will I put on a smile and a sense of calm as we give our daughters their Valentine's Day cards and gifts?* I couldn't believe that on a day we make so significant and special, I had just received crushing and life-altering news. How could the day of love be turned into the day of a possible death sentence? Yet, why not on this day? After all, cancer doesn't discriminate or differentiate, choosing one day or one person over another.

I can die from this! I thought. *The disease that starts with a big "C." I have the disease that spreads, that eats away at people's bodies, that weakens and kills people. That took the life of my father and my grandmother. That made them both suffer terribly. How did this happen? How did it happen to me?*

On this day when I should have been contemplating a special card filled with sentiments of love from my husband, I was considering my mortality. When I should have been smelling a bouquet of tangerine-colored roses, fragrant and beautiful, I sat at my desk, staring at the notes from my conversation with the radiologist—words on a page declaring that my life would never be the same. Instead of savoring my favorite chewy, nutty chocolates, I sat with bile rising in my throat, tasting the bitterness of the direction my life had just taken.

But was it an accident that I was diagnosed on the day we associate with hearts and love? Was it such a surprise that my cancer showed up in my heart center? After all, how was my heart? What condition was it in really? And what did I carry within it?

Admittedly, my heart was filled with anger, resentment, hurt, depression, and a deep sense of discontent and disconnection—I'd been carrying these emotions and feelings for at least a few years now. I had lost the ability to feel joy about life, especially mine. I was going through the motions of each day, but without any sense of gratitude or elation about the life I was living. Since our move to Colorado, I'd become a hermit crab, in between homes, not feeling settled or comfortable in my own skin. Outwardly, all looked great—a big, beautiful home; two beautiful daughters; plenty of activities; and a husband who brought in ample income. Inwardly, though, I was withering, shriveling away, going deeper and deeper into my shell to keep from feeling the overwhelming grief and sadness of leaving my shell home in California—my birthplace and the birthplace of our daughters—and moving to a new shell in Colorado at fifty years of age. The uncertainty of what to do to make my life better plagued me.

Even more frightening was the hint of *knowing* that I carried inside. I was not prepared for what I might need to do. It was hard to admit that I was feeling the overwhelming responsibility to keep our family afloat emotionally and psychologically, yet I was filled with fear and resentment. Almost four years after Dominic had to give up his identity, his vocation, and his hobby—his entire aviation career—with the pronouncement of an ischemic heart, he was still angry and grieving. We'd moved to a new state so he could find work in aviation, but having traded a cockpit for a cubicle was not working for him. He hated his job and vented almost daily. I did my best to keep my thoughts and feelings stuffed down, knowing that anytime I tried to offer suggestions or possible solutions to his suffering, I got shut down. Our daughters felt and witnessed his anguish yet didn't understand why he couldn't accept things the way they were or why I wasn't willing to make changes so they could feel a sense of peace and calm. Because I was not emotionally or financially ready for other significant life changes, such as separating from Dominic—and because I believed he could and would come to terms with the life changes we'd made in order to try and find a new path for him and our family—I wasn't ready to give up.

Our girls had never wanted to move—they'd been against it from the start—so they were angry too. Our trips to Colorado to

find a home and reconnect with their aunt—my sister, Debbie—
didn't seem to help. They continued to express how unhappy they
were before, during, and after our move. Since they didn't see their
dad doing any better, and maybe even doing worse emotionally,
they hated our new home state and our home. Although the move
meant they each had their own bedroom and we all had much
more personal space and areas for entertainment and creative projects, it didn't matter. They just wanted to go *home!* Even the new
family puppy didn't seem to ease their pain.

So, I continued to limp along. As beautiful as our new home
was, joy eluded me. After the girls went to bed at night, I took
baths to soothe and cleanse my body and spirit. I read. I played
piano. I focused on my family, attempting to grow roots for our
new life. I pasted a smile on my face and told everyone that we
could be happy if we just gave our new life a chance. And yet I
couldn't find any real sense of joy. I told myself I was happy—I
went through the motions to begin to build connections for all
of us. But deep within lay a shroud of darkness, sorrow, and pain
I couldn't shake off. It had been with me for most of my life and
hadn't stayed behind when I left California. Now, it was amplified
as I tried to deny its existence amid our current circumstances.

Although I attempted to put on a happy face for the three of
them, I was grieving too. I missed our California life. I missed our
routine. I missed teaching piano and continuing to take lessons
myself. I missed our homeschooling community and the additional
activities the girls had participated in with public school friends. I
missed their musical theater group and our voice lessons. I missed
their piano classes and their piano teacher with whom I'd become

friends. I missed our park days, hanging out with longtime friends and fellow homeschoolers. I missed my book club and tea with close friends. I missed all the women I'd leaned on as Dominic and I struggled to accept that he would never fly again. I missed my circle of support that expanded to fifty miles away—my closest women friends and my immediate family. All had been left behind. I told the girls we were expanding our circle with the new friends and activities and life we would create in Colorado, but every night in the privacy of my bedroom, as the girls slept and before Dominic got home from his swing shift job, I grieved. Sometimes I allowed myself to cry, but mostly I just felt an immense and overwhelming sadness.

Now my heart felt an additional burden and the need to face all I'd been trying to run from. It cried out with the pronouncement of breast cancer: *Will you listen now? Will you admit that all is not well with you? Will you finally begin to tend to your deeper self? Will you now be willing to care for yourself? Will you now express how* you *feel? Are you ready to stop pretending, to stop trying to make everything and everyone okay? Are you ready to admit that you can't fix everything, that you can't make everything and everyone better, that you can't save everyone from their pain, their fears, their grief? Is this what it took to get your attention?*

No, on this Valentine's Day, I didn't receive cards, or flowers, or a candlelight dinner. I did, however, receive a message that it was time to start paying attention. To start honoring myself and my needs. To start getting honest with myself and others. To start creating a life of my choosing, no matter how the rest of my family reacted. To start figuring out how to love me in the midst of chaos and crisis. Was I ready to begin? No, not really. But I could at least set the package called "start" on a shelf and know it was there waiting for me. I could remind myself that eventually, if I chose to do so, I could begin to make changes.

Happy Valentine's Day, Donna!

Why Me?

T his seems to be the universal question when life-shattering events happen—when we experience loss of some kind—a death, a divorce, a letting go we weren't ready for, a horrendous situation we never anticipated or imagined for ourselves. "Why me?" we ask. "Why now? Why this?"

I asked these unanswerable questions, even taking them a step further. *Why not her? Why not them? Why not a childless person or an old person or a person who isn't sure they even want to live anymore? Why not in twenty years or in a different lifetime? I have two eleven-year-old daughters to raise. They need me. I need them. Why me, God? Why now?*

A person can get stuck in the questions. The pleas, disbelief, denial, bargaining, and suffering can become a swirling vortex of mire we can't escape. They can turn into an internal scream that won't be silenced—a rage so big that we lose ourselves in the intense emotional whirlpool of pain and grief and can't find our way out. For a while, I was there—spiraling further into a deep, dark abyss I might never escape. I didn't voice out loud to anyone any of what was going on internally. I didn't dare allow myself to do that, but within the privacy of my mind, I negotiated with the Universe to find a way out. Most of my bargaining chips involved someone else having cancer rather than me. I'm not proud that I was willing to inflict others for the sake of my own health, but in the middle of the night, as I researched the "what if" scenarios of a cancer diagnosis, I was desperate to not have any of it be true and related to me. "Take them, not me!" I begged. "Please don't let this be true. Please let this be a terrible mistake," I pleaded.

One night, after everyone else was asleep and I'd been researching the statistics and life expectancy based on the various stages of cancer, I called my best friend, Denise, and her husband in California. It was around midnight PST when I dialed their number. "I'm scared I'll die," I cried into the phone. "I don't want to die! I want to see the girls grow up. If this is stage 4, I may not live that long. The statistics are not good."

"Stop!" my girlfriend commanded. "Stop researching. Stop reading online. Just like when I took the pregnancy books away from you while you were carrying the girls, you've got to stop this. This will not help you in any way."

I thought about what she'd done twelve years earlier. When we discovered that Baby B's growth had slowed down and fallen way behind her twin, Baby A, I started looking up every *what if* scenario, every possible *if this is the cause, then this can happen* description of what might be happening and what could possibly go wrong. At twenty-nine weeks' gestation, based on an extensive Doppler study that showed the significance of the slower growth for Baby B, my doctor put me in the hospital on bed rest. Before I was admitted, my girlfriend confiscated all my pregnancy books so I wouldn't be able to continue reading about possible horrendous outcomes.

Bringing me back to the call, her husband chimed in. "None of us knows how much time we have. Any of us could die tomorrow. So, it's about how you live each day. Are you going to live in fear of death, which won't be living at all, or will you do what's necessary and live for whatever amount of time you have left?"

His words shook me to my core. They didn't feel at all comforting. They actually scared me even more. "So, you're saying I might die from this?" I asked as the sobbing continued. I wanted to know outcomes; I wanted guarantees, whether good or bad. I wanted facts and truths so I could prepare.

"No, I'm saying none of us knows what tomorrow will bring. So live. Live every day as best you can. Deal with whatever you have to deal with and keep going for as long as you have, whether that's one day, one month, one year, one decade, or long into old age."

I began to breathe more slowly. It was one of the few times I'd allowed myself to cry, so it took a while to stop the flow of tears. By the time we hung up, I was calmer. No one had a crystal ball, and all I could do was try my best to live rather than tell myself I was dying.

Slowly, I began to crawl out of that deep sinkhole I'd slipped into. As the days passed, my pleading and bargaining and anger quieted down. In time, I came to, *Why not me? What makes me so special to think this couldn't happen to me? And who knows how this will turn out?*

I was finally able to see that I'm a garden-variety human being, no different than anyone else, no more special than the people all around me. My life is no more significant or valuable than any other person's, even those who aren't sure they want to continue to be here. It is not my call, nor up to any other person, to decide the value of any one individual's life. A life has been given to those of us who walk this planet, and it's up to us to decide how we'll use it—it's ours to do with as we choose. I can choose to get stuck here in all the *what ifs* and *why mes*, or I can choose to go on. I can choose to live until my final breath.

In the subsequent months, I chose life and faced the journey in front of me. For however long, in whatever form my life would take, ultimately, I chose me. But getting there took time—a very long time.

So Many Choices

For those of us who possess the financial means and are connected to available resources, choices are everywhere, even in the most mundane circumstances. *Which shoes do I want? Which dress looks best? What color should I dye my hair? Which car or television do we want? Which electronic device? Apple or Microsoft? Android or iPhone? Where do we want to live, and which house should we buy?* The choices are endless. I am fortunate to have so many options available. Yet, choices can be paralyzing too—they can make one unable to move in any direction.

After my diagnosis, I discovered I had unlimited choices available to me—choices that went far beyond which oncologist and surgeon to work with. Would I follow conventional treatment? If I did, would I have a mastectomy or lumpectomy? Would I have radiation or chemo? Would I take oral medication for five years following surgery? Or would I do some combination?

And what about alternative methods? So many types of alternative therapies and variations of each existed! Body work, energy work, nutritional options, supplements, infusions, mental practices, cleanses for the body and mind, and more. The list of choices was exhausting and overwhelming—sometimes exasperatingly confusing.

Which ones should I choose? What combos will be best? Which protocol might be most successful? I was desperate to find *just the right thing*, yet I became immobile. I couldn't decide. I couldn't choose. I just *couldn't!*

Then there were the "experts" who provided all those options, which made the act of choosing even more difficult. *Who is right? Who is wrong? Who is lying or embellishing the truth, and who truly cares? Who has the best advice, the right plan, the* real answer? *Who has the* cure?

I got stuck, not only in a crisis of what to choose but also in how to decide which "side" was right. I needed to determine which camp I'd align with. I soon found myself in an "us versus them" place, a zone filled with conflict, misunderstanding, confusion, and distrust of *the other* from both sides. I had entered the *in between*—a place riddled with landmines—and I didn't know where to step.

The last thing I needed as I considered how to heal myself was conflict in the form of skepticism, loathing, distrust, judgment, or blame. My body was already in an internal conflict, which my mind had joined, and my angst and feelings of uncertainty and even doom became amplified. As I looked for answers from those who were supposed to "above all else, do no harm," I got caught in the crossfire. Like a deer in headlights, I froze. And, although I knew I was incredibly fortunate to have so many options available to me—and possessed the ability to choose whatever I wanted for myself—I stayed incapable of movement for quite some time.

Two Perky Breasts ... or Not

When I first met the surgeon, I was struck by her physique and appearance. Tall, attractive, full-figured, muscular, and tan. I found out she was a cyclist. She had the most beautiful smile of any doctor I'd ever met, and she appeared confident. She exuded self-assurance and knowing, so much so that I was taken aback. A force to be reckoned with. Although I held back emotionally, I sensed I would be in good hands if I chose to work with her.

As with all doctors, however, I approached her and our first appointment with skepticism and caution. Even though she looked *safe enough,* initially, I didn't deal with her any differently than other new doctors I'd encountered.

She smiled and sat down behind her desk, inviting me to sit across from her. Clue #1—the desk of separation—a symbol of who was in charge, who was the authority. I said that I was there to gather information. I wasn't sure I was ready to do anything more.

"Yes, I see from the images that the area identified so far is small. You may be a candidate for a lumpectomy," she began.

"I don't plan to have a lumpectomy," I replied. "I don't want to undergo radiation, which I know is the standard of care." The ball was back in her court.

"Yes, it is. So, then you're contemplating a mastectomy?"

"Yes," I responded.

"Well, then, you have some options here. You can use this surgery to have the breasts you've always wanted. Bigger, perkier ones that will never sag or droop. They'll stay perky for the rest of your life." She lit up even brighter as she invited me to dream.

"I'm not interested in bigger breasts," I explained.

"Well, I had one patient who removed both breasts and didn't do reconstruction. She's a cyclist and didn't want them getting in the way when she rode. She'd been rather large-breasted."

"I honestly like my breasts just as they are. I hate the thought of losing even one, and I'm definitely not interested in removing the other electively," I added.

She paused. I could tell she was considering the type of person sitting before her. I believe she was beginning to see that I wasn't going to just go along with the program, whatever that prescribed course of action might be.

"Well, we can remove the one breast, and you could have reconstruction, where we'd match it up to your other breast as best we could. They would never be an exact match. I want you to know that upfront, but by doing reconstruction, you'd have two breasts."

"I really don't want to undergo reconstruction. Multiple surgeries, procedures, and more healing. If I do have a mastectomy, that will be it. I don't want to compromise my immune system any further."

"You could have a tattoo done afterward. A butterfly maybe. I've had patients who did that, and they looked and felt beautiful. You could also opt to have reconstruction down the road. That can always be an option should you decide you want to have it done later."

I was getting the message that she thought something should be done to make the area attractive. I wondered if maybe she really did think I'd look ugly and disfigured from a mastectomy.

"So how does it look after a mastectomy is done? I saw my grandmother's when I was a young girl, and I recall how dimply the area looked. She also had a gigantic scar. Do they look better now?" I asked. I described more about how my grandmother's chest had looked.

"She had a radical mastectomy, which was the only option in the sixties, and very traumatic. What you'll undergo is nothing like that. Here, I can show you a diagram. I also have photos of some of my patients who volunteered to be included in my book."

It was like shopping for a new car. Options, levels of service, add-ons, and extras—even photos to look at.

She showed me the diagram. The picture depicted a little half-moon scar, shorter in length than the width of the breast area, centered where the nipple had been. *That wouldn't be so bad actually,* I thought to myself. *Better looking than I imagined.* I could tell she was waiting for my response. "That looks nice," I acquiesced. "I think I can live with that."

After more discussion about the procedure and the next steps in preparation for surgery, I left with her book, paperwork, and a surgery date less than a month away. Within days, I canceled the surgery date to begin the quest for another solution. It turned out I wasn't ready to proceed with an option that would be so *final*.

The greatest gift she gave me when I told her of my decision to hold off on a mastectomy was, "You have time. This is not an aggressive cancer, and you can take time to decide what is right for you. Above all else, you need to feel and know you've made the right decision. Your decision has to be the right one for you."

So, she had understood me after all. She had "gotten" me. And she had just handed me the most important piece of the puzzle— the gift of time.

No!

We sat at the kitchen table for dinner—my father, mother, sister, and me. My father asked me to pass the butter to him. "No!" I answered. I was busy eating my food, and, at five years old, I saw no reason to have to stop. In my innocence, I had answered him honestly. No, I couldn't pass what he wanted because I was hungry. I couldn't stop to help him out. I wanted to eat my food.

My next memory is of being hit—backhanded across my cheek and knocked off my chair. I lay there—shocked, startled, and scared. *What did I do wrong? Why did Daddy strike me?* Years later, I would learn that my father got up from the table and went into the only bathroom in our two-bedroom home, where he cried. He never let us see his tears, his regret, his remorse, or his sorrow. And he never apologized.

That night, I learned the first of many lessons about how to behave. First and foremost was to never say no to the adults in my life.

In 2007, when I was diagnosed, everyone assumed I would rush off to surgery. After all, wasn't that the normal course of action to get the unwanted invader removed as quickly as possible? To render the attacker powerless?

Dominic expected that I'd immediately take care of it and do whatever was necessary to ensure that the cancer was eradicated, especially since we had two young daughters who needed me. Everyone—family, friends, and doctors—assumed the same.

But I shocked them all, and even surprised myself, when I proclaimed a very loud "No!"

I wanted time to digest what was happening to me. I wanted to understand and study my options. Weren't there more choices out there beyond surgery? I wanted to give myself the gift of considering those options. Most of all, I wanted to decide for myself—not take action because of what others expected from me or told me to do.

My five-year-old self had complied out of necessity. Being a good girl had been the way to not only survive but to thrive in childhood. It was how I received acknowledgment and even love. Life had been conditional as a child—to gain approval and acceptance, I had to do my best to conform.

Through the years, I'd stifled many nos. I pushed down my desires and my needs over and over during my childhood. Even as an adult, I frequently denied what I wanted in order to please others or avoid conflict. Breast cancer was my wake-up call. How often had I not let my voice be heard? How often had I not expressed myself—my needs, my desires, my concerns, and even my fears? How many times had I suppressed those thoughts and feelings in order to not make waves in an attempt to make others feel more comfortable?

My fifty-one-year-old "no" was the beginning of allowing my truth to rise to the surface and pour out of me. It was the beginning of expressing more of me—who I was and what I wanted. It was the start of giving myself permission to search for the meaning of this woman's life.

"No" opened the doors. Actually, "no" opened the floodgates to finding my way home, back to me.

The Ability to Choose

I didn't always have the ability to choose. Especially as a child—my parents, school, church, and community dictated what I could or couldn't do. From a very young age, I learned that my voice didn't matter; my needs and wants were secondary, or unimportant, to others, most especially adults. I would have to do what I was told, and that was the way it was.

The first such moment I can remember happened when I was about three and a half years old. It was naptime, and I lay in my bed next to my eighteen-month-old sister, who was in her crib. Debbie pulled herself up at the side of her crib and threw out her glass bottle. Still containing milk, it hit the hard linoleum floor and shattered, splattering milk everywhere. In between our two beds was my most special "toy," a giant stuffed pink poodle. It, along with the floor, took the brunt of the flying milk and shards of glass. My father had won the giant poodle for me at a local carnival.

Dad was an expert dime-tosser and almost always walked away from any dime-toss booth with at least one prize, oftentimes the biggest and grandest. My stuffed pink poodle was the first prize I can remember him winning for me. I loved and cherished it. The dog was as big as I was, maybe bigger. Seeing it sprayed with milk and glass, I began to scream.

Hearing all the commotion in our room, my mother came running. She shrieked once she saw what had happened, worried initially that one of us was hurt. She told me to stay in bed so I wouldn't get cut by the broken glass scattered throughout the center aisle of our floor. Then she began to clean up the mess.

Mom worked methodically, sweeping up the glass and wiping down everything—walls, floor, crib rails, and our bedside table. Then she looked over at my poodle and said it needed to be thrown away. I began to cry. *How can she do that? And how could Debbie make me lose my beautiful dog? If Daddy were here, I'm sure this would never happen. He'd find a way to save it.*

My mom tried to calm my hysteria and explain that she could not clean the dog properly and ensure that all the glass was removed from its fur. I sobbed, unable to fathom that I was about to lose my first big toy—my most prized possession.

Pleading with her, I tried to change her mind. I begged, but nothing worked. I watched as she left the room, carrying away my beautiful stuffed pink poodle. Devastated, I knew it would never come back to my room again. I looked over at my baby sister and told her I'd be mad at her forever. Although I couldn't express in words that she'd just ruined my life, those were my feelings. I felt crushed. I screamed at her and then continued to bawl into my pillow.

She was an easy target. Who I really wanted to yell at was my mother, but I knew if I did that or if I said mean things to my mom, I'd most likely get spanked. So rather than risk physical pain, I lashed out at my baby sister. I continued to cry until I had no more tears left.

In that moment, it seemed that what I wanted didn't matter. I believed that my mother didn't care about me. She never came back to hold me or try to console me in my sadness. She never tried to do anything to make the hurt go away or to make me feel better. Once the mess was cleaned up, it was time to go on with our day—to get up from our naps, get dressed, and play while Mommy prepared dinner. There would be no more crying or whining. No more revisiting what had happened, not even when my father got home. My carnival poodle was gone. The matter was over. End of story. Period.

The next big moment I can remember when I had no say in a matter happened prior to the time I started kindergarten. I'll never forget "the haircut."

As a little girl, I loved my hair. I had straight, shoulder-length hair that my mother curled for special occasions. Sometimes, she'd put barrettes and headbands and ribbons in my hair. When it was all fixed up, I felt like a princess.

After Debbie was born, my mom took the two of us for "sister" photos on at least two occasions. At the time of the second photo,

Debbie was two and I was four years old. That photo is one of my most treasured possessions. There we sit with big smiles on our faces, wearing straight bangs while the rest of our hair is curly.

Around four years old, my mother took me to the beauty shop, and I got my first perm. My mom had it done so that my hair could be curly (maybe emulating Shirley Temple's childhood hairstyle) without her having to put curlers in my hair at night. I know I didn't like sleeping on them, not even the soft, squishy pink foam rubber ones. I was excited to have curly hair, especially after the beautician showed me a magazine picture of how my hair would look. As she squeezed the bottle and applied the perm solution all over my head, it stunk and made my eyes water, but I didn't complain one bit. The pretty curls I would end up with were well worth the temporary discomfort.

After the treatment, and after sitting in the hairdryer chair atop a stack of telephone books so my head was inside the bubble hairdryer, my curls were set. The beautician helped me back into her styling chair and handed me a mirror. She swung me around so I could see my hair on the sides and in back. I loved my curls. Now I could be a princess forever.

My curls started just above my ears and traveled all the way to my shoulders. They bounced when I jumped up and down. They scrunched in my hands and sprung forward when I released them. I felt pretty with my headful of beautiful curls. I wanted to have curly hair forever. Unfortunately, some months later, that would all change.

Late in the summer of the year I turned five, my mother decided my hair should be cut short. Pixies were popular—the no-care, easy-to-manage hairstyle of the day. It would make my mom's life easier not having to tend to my hair each day, especially since I would soon be starting school. I would even be able to take care of it myself.

My mother scheduled the appointment on a day when my father was home so he could watch my three-year-old sister; however, I let my parents know that I didn't want the haircut. I protested. I begged. I pleaded. "Please don't make me get a haircut! Please! I want long hair. I don't want short hair," I cried, but it didn't matter.

Off we went. My mother told me that I'd like it after it was cut. I cried all the way to the little one-bedroom house where the beauty shop was located. When I got in the chair and sat up on the booster, I wouldn't sit still the way I had for my perm. I squirmed. I kicked. I whimpered and cried. Finally, the beautician told my mother that she wouldn't be able to cut my hair unless I calmed down. Frustrated, embarrassed, and unable to convince me to be quiet, my mother took me home. My father met us in the basement and sat me on the washing machine. In a very stern voice, he stated, "If you don't stop crying and knock off this behavior and let the beautician cut your hair, you're going to get a real good spanking from me."

I didn't want that, and I knew he was mad enough that I would definitely get punished by him. So, I closed my mouth, stopped crying, and silently got into the car with my mom. As the tears quietly ran down my cheeks, my mother drove us back to the beauty shop. Once the beautician helped me up onto the booster seat in her hairdresser chair and put the cape around me, I sat as still as possible and didn't say another word. I tried my best not to cry, although a few tears did trickle down my face. I didn't smile or make any sounds of protest. No one tried to talk to me either.

Defeated, I continued to sit upright and only moved my head when instructed by the beautician. My parents had decided what would happen without any consideration of what I wanted for myself. Apparently, it didn't matter what I wanted. As my hair slid down the cape and fell to the floor, so did any hope I'd been holding that they would listen to me.

It would be years before I'd try so hard to be heard again. By then, I'd be a teenager who was more willing to risk the ire of my parents and no longer afraid that I'd get spanked. By then, that "parenting technique" was no longer used in our home. At least for a time, I didn't worry about what they thought or did in response to my demands.

That rebellious teenager eventually settled down and, for the most part, disappeared into acquiescence. She only reappeared when the stakes seemed to be especially high, but her appearances were few and far between. My cancer diagnosis was the event that brought the adult version of her to life—this time, willing and ready to do battle with anyone who got in her way.

Did I Cause It?

Although I wouldn't admit it to anyone, and most definitely not to myself, I was *desperate* to find a way to rid myself of cancer without the need for Western medicine. I was willing to try just about anything and spend almost any amount of money to avoid traditional approaches to cancer treatment. But what? And with whom? And how much money or how far away was I willing to go? To another state? Another country? I started with my local health store and bought glass bottles full of supplements and elixirs to build my immune system and detox my body. I bought so many that within weeks, I gagged and almost immediately threw them back up as I tried to get the fistfuls down three times a day.

I sought the help of a local practitioner and began to try various detoxing techniques. I met with a nutritionist who specialized in working with people who had cancer. I met with energy practitioners and a chiropractor and sampled every practice and concoction they suggested. I cleaned up my diet and began to drop weight as a result of cutting out all grains except ancient grains, all dairy, all meat, and all sugar. I quit all caffeine except for green tea. I began biofeedback. I read books to understand other healing modalities, searching for more options to try. I watched videos by two women who had *cured themselves* of cancer and practiced the daily living lifestyle they taught, hoping my behaviors would make the cancer go away. I even tried to find a miracle healing salve that was supposed to draw tumors right out of my body. I was willing to try anything to kill and excise the cancer, anything that would keep me away from radiation, surgery, and chemotherapy—the burn, slash, and poison "solutions."

I was like a bouncing ball as I went from one person, one idea, and one behavior to another. Each discovery revealed more paths, and before long, I had a collection of over twenty books, multiple DVDs, a pantry and refrigerator full of healthy foods and supplements, and a calendar filled with daily appointments.

I wouldn't recognize it for what it was until much later, but one of the hidden blessings I received during this maddening quest was a conversation I had with one particular energy healer. She asked me, "What happened in your life about three years ago? Almost always, there's a traumatic event around that timeframe that is the catalyst for cancer."

"Well," I replied, "my husband lost his aviation career in 2003 due to an ischemic heart, and after appealing the FAA's decision, with the support of his cardiologist and a cardiac surgeon, he was told the decision was final. He would not ever be able to fly again. He was devastated—we all were. With that verdict, we decided to move to Colorado at the end of 2005. He and I were fifty years old and our daughters were ten. None of us was 100 percent enthused about such a drastic life change, but for a variety of reasons, it seemed to make sense. Could that be the reason?"

I told her more about the emotional state of our family at the time and all I'd done to try to maintain homeostasis within our home over these past four years. I disclosed to her how, by trying to be there for everyone else, I pushed down my fears, my anger, and my grief. There didn't seem to be any space for what I was going through.

"Yes, I am sure all of that added up to your disease. Stress suppresses the immune system, as you know. It's been scientifically proven. And you were obviously under a tremendous amount of stress. Add to that your need to support your husband and daughters by denying your own feelings ... by stuffing them down ... the immune system gets even more compromised. Your body became fertile ground for cancer to thrive."

I'd considered my diet and poor eating habits, including all the white sugar and white flour we'd consumed in the past. Comfort foods. Even though we'd been eating organic foods for almost a decade, I still had been eating plenty of "junk" and processed foods. I'd thought about all the water drunk out of store-bought plastic bottles. I'd looked at all our daily personal care and household items. All of it added up to environmental contributors to cancer, and I'd since gotten rid of every possible culprit. We even added water filters to the house to eliminate chlorine.

However, until this conversation, I'd never looked at the ways in which I'd overtaxed my body as a result of my emotional and psychological struggles. One reason I'm sure I never looked too deeply was that this area would be much more difficult to address. This would require looking at lifelong family patterns that I'd continued in my immediate family. How would I ever begin to tell the truth about my current thoughts and feelings since I'd learned early on that they didn't matter? It was relatively easy to gulp down supplements and eliminate certain foods and beverages from my diet, but how would I ever begin to express everything I'd kept hidden for so long? And how would I ever forgive myself for not being willing to get honest? Had my need to hide my truth caused me to manifest cancer? Did I cause my cancer? I didn't like the answers I initially got when I asked myself these questions.

If Only

Thinking that I might have caused my cancer took me to my knees. *What have I done?* I wondered. Why hadn't I been more honest and upfront about my feelings, especially to myself, after Dominic was permanently grounded? Why did I convince myself—and everyone else who was concerned about such a huge life change for our family—that I was okay with moving out of state? Why had I denied that I was terrified at the thought of moving to Colorado?

Our family had experienced an event that would impact our lives forever. The loss of Dominic's aviation career was a blow that forced us to look at how and where we would live in the future. We looked at everything that was affected by the loss of an income we'd come to rely on, including whether I needed to return to work. While feeling devastated as we watched the trajectory of our family's life go in a direction we never anticipated, we made decisions, especially the decision to move to Colorado, thinking they were best for all of us.

Everything I did or didn't do in response to these life-altering decisions had been from a place of love. It might have been a distorted version of love, but I'd acted from my heart to protect my family from my fear and my anger at the loss of Dominic's career. I didn't want to cause Dominic further suffering—he was struggling enough already. And I was determined to show our daughters that we could survive the changes and even thrive in our lives in a new home state. So, I'd put on a mask of courage, strength, support, and trust that we were doing the right thing for our family.

For my own benefit, I had needed to maintain some sense of control in a somewhat out-of-control situation. That required me to "act as if" and keep myself from acknowledging my feelings as much as possible. And that is what I had done. I didn't allow myself much time to consider my feelings—not when my family needed me.

This was a familiar role because hadn't I learned to do that as a small child? Hadn't there been an unspoken message in my family of origin that Daddy's feelings had to be protected and that Daddy needed to know we loved him no matter what? It didn't matter how I felt, especially when it came to feelings of fear. If Daddy had done something wrong and Mommy was mad at Daddy, especially if he'd gotten drunk and embarrassed her at a family holiday or party with friends, it was important for me to tell Daddy how much I loved him. Somehow, I'd internalized a message that it was up to me to make sure Daddy was okay—somehow that became my role and made me feel safer too. No matter what, when Daddy was feeling remorse for his behavior and Mommy wouldn't accept his apologies, I had to let Daddy know that I loved him and would always be there for him.

Now, in my immediate family, I felt responsible for making sure Dominic and our daughters were okay. So, a lifelong pattern was reactivated, along with all the suppressed fears of safety and security that were triggered within me. It didn't matter how I felt or what I thought—it only mattered that my family felt loved and that I helped us all manage the current storm. There was no time or place for my feelings—it was time for action. In the process of ensuring that they felt loved, safe, and secure, I'd become clogged up with all I pushed down.

Coming to these realizations didn't dissolve my cancer. It did help me, though, to talk myself down from a ledge every time I started the blame game all over again. I wasn't at a place of self-compassion or self-forgiveness, but at least I stopped chastising myself for having cancer.

And, as much as I wish it had, these realizations didn't make me change my behavior. I was still dealing with the cancer residing in my body. This cancer was real, and I was aware that it might still be growing. I needed to find the right solutions for my treatment. As I continued to look for an answer to eliminate my cancer, I continued to keep my thoughts and feelings, fears and concerns, to myself. I continued to pretend that I had everything under control—that I was *in* control and didn't need anything from anyone else, including my family.

If only it had been true.

An Easier, Softer Way?

My search for another option to eliminate my cancer seemed to be a search for a solution that wouldn't hurt me, cause me more harm, or disfigure me; in retrospect, I think it was more about needing to be *in control* of my destiny. In an out-of-control situation, I wanted to be the one in the driver's seat, no matter how crazy the possible solutions I considered. For instance, I was willing to look at alternatives with unknown outcomes and even the potential for creating more damage to my body. One of those "solutions" was black salve.

I'd been told about it by a woman I met with—a woman who believed that good alternatives usually remained underground. In late April, she had performed my thermography exam—another way to do imaging that didn't expose me to radiation. I hoped the thermogram would show that the cancer had been eliminated.

Instead, it indicated "hot spots" at my right breast and my lymph nodes leading to my armpit. Confirmation that I likely still had cancer and that it might have spread. In early May, I had a second ultrasound; I needed to know if those "lit up" red hot spots meant that the cancer had spread.

The female radiologist who was working the day of my second ultrasound came into the room to speak to me about her findings—a practice radiologists don't usually initiate. "I think it may have spread to your lymph nodes," she said with the look and sound of deep concern. "I think it's really in your best interests to consult with your surgeon. I honestly don't think it's safe for you to continue to wait to address this."

Even after the radiologist told me this, I still wasn't ready to return to my surgeon. That's when I remembered the black salve.

I contacted the woman who said she could get it and asked to meet with her privately. When we met, she provided me with the salve and instructions for what to do—how to apply it, how long to leave it on, and what to expect when the cancer was literally "pulled" from my body. It wasn't going to be a pretty picture as the tumor(s) would come up from under my skin and break the surface to finally "fall away." Somehow, though, in my mind, this seemed *better* than undergoing surgery. I could keep my breast, and I wouldn't need to undergo radiation or chemotherapy as I would if I had a lumpectomy. My lymph nodes would remain undisturbed, which was still important to me—no matter what the first radiologist had said.

With the salve and instructions in hand, I headed to the store and bought all the paraphernalia I would need: popsicle sticks for applying the salve, gauze pads for bandaging, adhesive tape, gloves, and alcohol wipes to keep everything germ-free. I was ready to do it—to extricate the cancer.

Not knowing how big the tumor was, or if there was more than one, I had no way of knowing what would come through or how big a hole it would create. Would it leave a crater or a tiny wound that would scab over and heal? I didn't know, but I wouldn't let myself think too much about what would come next. My mission, my primary goal, was to use a treatment that didn't involve Western medicine.

My disdain for Western medicine was difficult to understand and, most significantly, challenging to explain—especially since Western medicine had saved Dominic's life in 1996. Had he not driven himself to the ER on the day of our daughters' six-month "birthday," had the on-duty cardiologist not performed an angiogram a day later that revealed multiple arterial occlusions, one of which was over 95 percent occluded, and had he not undergone quintuple bypass surgery four days after that, Dominic would not have lived. Once he was home recovering, as we watched the news late one night, we learned about a male figure skater who dropped dead due to an occlusion. This could have been Dominic's outcome had he not listened to his body that Sunday morning in January while mowing the lawn.

Six months earlier, in July 1995, Western medicine had also saved our daughters, who were born by cesarean section eight weeks early. Had I not been hospitalized and monitored for three weeks prior to their birth, after discovering that Baby B was not growing in utero, and had they not seen the fetal distress that she was exhibiting just days before their birth, our girls might not have made it safely into the world.

So why did I have so little trust in Western medicine when it came to cancer? The answers were hard to discover, hidden by decades of scabbed-over fear and grief, but they were there: Because, as a teenager, I had watched my grandmother suffer, wither away, and die. And, as an adult, I had witnessed my father become weaker and weaker while doing everything he could to be involved in his granddaughters' lives until they were twenty-two months old.

It had been my father's spirit that kept us from seeing how much he was suffering and made it difficult for me to acknowledge just how sick he was. When he decided he could no longer endure the inward daily striving to stay alive and the chemotherapy treatments that he silently had undergone for over three years, he died within a few days. Until then, I'd continued to believe my dad would get better. In the family home where I'd grown up, he took his last breath at sixty-seven years old.

As I contemplated what I was about to do, I believed it was a better option than anything Western medicine could offer me. I didn't have faith that the traditional approaches would cure my cancer and save my life. Except for my mother's successful lumpectomy the previous year, I had no evidence I could point to that proved people could be "cured." And she was less than a year out from her procedure, so it was too early to use that term relative to her outcome. The only cases I'd heard about that actually used the word "cure" were from alternative methods. I decided to continue down this path.

A few days later, on a morning in the third week of May, I was finally ready to proceed. I went through the process I'd been instructed to follow. Wash the area, dry it, then use the alcohol wipes to sterilize the area, all while wearing gloves. Next, use the wooden stick to extract the salve from the jar. Apply the salve in a thick coating over the entire area of my breast, all the way to my armpit, cover with nonstick gauze pads, tape, and then put on my bra. The salve would immediately go to work to heat up and pull out the tumor. It would take about forty-eight hours. Seventy-two at most.

Three days passed as I waited, looked at my breast for any changes, showered each day, reapplied the salve, and waited some more. Nothing changed. I didn't feel anything happening, and my breast looked exactly the same. There were no physical sensations and no redness that was supposed to appear as the salve heated things up internally. Why wasn't it working?

I called my source to let her know what *wasn't* happening. She had no answers or suggestions other than to give it a couple more days. She finally told me that maybe what she'd been provided wasn't the "real thing," but where she'd gotten it should have been a reliable "supplier."

After two more days, I had to admit that I'd been given a dud—or an impostor. My breast tissue looked as pale white as ever. I didn't feel tingling or burning or any sensations to indicate that changes were happening under the surface.

I was totally defeated. Everything I'd tried had failed me. Everything! Supplements, elixirs, dietary changes, guided meditation, visualization, energy work, and now black salve—none of it had reversed or eradicated my cancer. I was in the same place

I'd been more than three months earlier—maybe even in a worse place. The radiologist had certainly thought so. Yet, I recalled what the surgeon had told me. She believed I could take the time to find my answers and the right direction. She hadn't advocated for an alternative to surgery, but she supported that I could take the time I needed. Of course, with the expectation that I'd come back to surgery wholeheartedly.

Frustrated, scared, and utterly hopeless, I cried as I dumped my brown-handled bag and all of its miracle contents in the garbage can. It had turned out to be fake.

At an all-time low, I couldn't even begin to think about what to do next. That evening, as I sat in my bedroom crying, I felt the world of hope, optimism, and endless possibilities fading. Like the sun setting outside my window, my dreams of alternative therapies were vanishing before my eyes. I felt betrayed and abandoned— and completely alone. I didn't want to admit that I'd come to the end of the road, but I had no other ideas, no other people to seek out, no other miracle cures to investigate, and no other sources for another way.

But was that really true?

As I continued to cry, I suddenly remembered a book I'd purchased that talked about facilities that offered alternative treatment modalities. I pulled the book from my shelf and started thumbing through it. The following morning, I began making phone calls, which led to other calls. I was referred to one center that was out of state and seemed to have a *balanced* program—integrating diet with IV infusions, supplements, and spiritual practices. The drawback was the cost. It would require us to look for money to be able to pay for it. I wasn't going to let that stop me, so I began to seriously consider the possibility of taking out a loan against our home. But this would take time, and I was beginning to wonder if time was still on my side. Additionally, I would have to be *accepted* into their program, and I wasn't sure my condition would qualify.

The world seemed to be against me. At every turn, I was hitting roadblocks or struggling with failed attempts. Why weren't my efforts leading to the results I'd envisioned for myself? Why wasn't I already cured—like some of the miracle stories I'd read about or watched in videos? Who or what had it in for me?

For a brief moment, I let myself live in the land of victimhood, completely forgetting my inner belief that doors close for reasons. Reasons that go beyond what I might be able to understand at the time. Looking back, I know I was actually being saved from my own desperation and fear—all of the doors that closed in my face forced me to look in other directions, including behind me. But at the time, I couldn't see that. All I saw was evidence that the world and the divine were conspiring against me.

I crumpled up the notes I'd been taking with each phone call and threw them on the ground as tears streamed down my face. "Why can't I find a solution? Why can't I find the way out? I don't want to have surgery!" I screamed.

If You Were My Wife ...

I thought back to the most recent appointment with the female radiologist. I had been devastated when she gave me her interpretations of my ultrasound. How had I ended up here? I hadn't been passive. I hadn't been sitting around, hoping that the cancer would miraculously disappear. I had been working hard to reverse my disease. I had done just about everything that was introduced or suggested to me during my search to find a way to avoid traditional treatments. Yet, it appeared that all my efforts to find a natural way to eradicate the cancer had failed—it seemed likely that in the course of the past few months, the cancer had actually spread.

Seeing how upset I was, the radiologist had put her hand on my shoulder and tried to comfort me. "You're going to be okay," she said.

Now I knew the real truth. It *was* too late. Everything, including the black salve, had failed me. And faraway treatment centers and clinics were just too expensive for us to manage without taking on exorbitant debt. But how could I ever be okay if I had to give in and subject myself to the methods I'd been trying to avoid? Surgery, chemo, and radiation all seemed as bad as a death sentence.

What do I do now? I thought as the tears flowed. *What now?*

"I don't know what to do!" I cried out to Dominic the following day. "Everything has failed me!"

Knowing that I needed to find peace for myself in whatever I ultimately did, after watching me scramble over the past twenty-four hours to find an affordable treatment center alternative, he looked me in the eyes and spoke, giving me the most selfless gift possible.

"You wanted to go to the Chopra Center *after* you were healed. I remember you telling me how it would help you heal further physically, mentally, and spiritually. Well, maybe you shouldn't wait. Why don't you go now? Maybe going through their five-day program will help you find the answers you've been searching for." His words and suggestion were more generous than anything I could have ever imagined receiving from him, especially since I knew he'd been struggling to understand my need to pursue so many different avenues during these past months. He'd watched me in a constant manic state as I flitted from one option to another, throwing money from our meager savings here and there and everywhere. I knew it hadn't been easy for him.

"Really?" I asked. "Do you think that might help?" I continued to sob.

"I don't know, but it's obvious that you've got to find a way to move forward and be okay with whatever you decide to do. No matter what I think, you've got to find your own answers. Maybe you'll find them there."

Although we were standing several feet from each other, no longer knowing how to console one another physically, I felt his words wash over me with a sense of generosity and deep love. *I need to call.*

It turned out that the Chopra Center was conducting their next five-day "Perfect Health" program the following week, and they just so happened to have *one opening. There are no accidents!* I reserved the spot and made my plane reservations. I would be departing in a few days, hopefully to find answers, a sense of peace, and a cure—and spending much less money than the alternative programs I'd considered.

As I made my way to the center, deep inside, I believed they would show me another way to excise the cancer without undergoing conventional treatment. Even while I was there, I continued to research and contemplate alternative avenues, hoping that either what I experienced at the center or my findings would eradicate my cancer.

During the five days, each attendee was scheduled to meet with one of the doctors on staff. I found out that because I had a diagnosis of cancer, I'd be meeting with Dr. David Simon, the head of the Chopra Center at the time, and Deepak's partner. I felt a mixture of excitement and fear as I contemplated meeting him on my first full day there. *What will he be like? What will he say? Will I feel comfortable meeting with him? I guess I should feel fortunate, but what if he's aloof or uncaring or pompous?* The thoughts went on and on as I awaited my appointment.

My appointment started with a physical exam followed by a face-to-face consultation. As Dr. Simon examined my breasts and my nearby lymph nodes, he said he believed my lymph nodes were clear and that the cancer was localized to my right breast. Once I got dressed and we sat down to talk, the first thing he asked was whether I'd read his book *A Return to Wholeness*. I had not. He told me to get it and read it while I was there. He then added, "If you were my wife, I'd take you immediately to the surgeon and schedule your surgery. And if you needed chemo or radiation, I'd insist that you do whatever was necessary to be healed." *Not the words I was expecting.*

He then explained that *A Return to Wholeness* was written on the premise that ancient medicine, such as Ayurveda, cannot alone cure our modern-day diseases. We need to take an integrative approach and incorporate the best from what ancient wisdom, modern medicine, and current science have to offer. He and Deepak Chopra were MDs who integrated all of them. He told me that once I read through his book, I'd see how I could bring in Ayurveda and integrative practices to support whatever I underwent through conventional treatment. At the end of our meeting, he reiterated that as soon as I got home, I needed to schedule that appointment with my surgeon.

I left his office reeling. I had expected him to tell me that after detoxing at the center and participating in their five-day regimen,

I'd be cured—or at least on my way. How naïve I was! I never anticipated that he would advocate conventional treatment. Needing to gain a better understanding of his beliefs and his advice, I immediately went to their on-site store and bought his book, one of the many he'd written by that time. That night, I started reading and finished it before the program came to an end.

His book and approach made sense, yet I could not come to terms with the idea of chemotherapy or radiation. I knew I would not have a lumpectomy, so radiation would, most likely, not be a part of my treatment. But chemotherapy was definitely a possibility if the cancer had spread to my lymph nodes. Although I felt nurtured by the week's routine of healthy food, detoxing, massages, yoga, morning and evening meditation, and daily lectures, I could not shake my growing internal fear. On the fourth morning, I had a chance to speak with the female physician who was available to us as part of our daily program. I told her about my deep-seated fear of chemo.

"I just don't know how I'll ever be able to see chemo as anything but poison that will destroy all the good in my body as well as the cancer."

She looked at me with deep compassion and told me about her family life, having been raised by two "alternative" doctors, and how, in the course of her own medical training, she'd come to see integration as the answer. She offered to give me her personal perspective on chemo, and I gladly accepted her gift, wanting to grab onto anything that might help me come to a resolution about the course ahead.

"I see chemo removing the cancerous cells and healthy cells along with it, which then creates a space for healing, vitality, wholeness, and health that isn't possible right now. I see it as creating a big open container, a clear vessel that you can then fill with everything that will support wellness. Through your food, supplements, spiritual practices, visualization, movement, and other daily practices, you can restore your body to perfect health."

I hadn't ever considered the picture she painted. I'd only seen chemo as a poison to be feared and avoided, a destroyer that leaves behind only devastation and destruction—an evil that is hard to recover from. After all, I'd watched my father die from the effects of chemo. What she described, though, was beautiful, talking about color and light and bringing in all of my senses to understand how this could be a gift in my life rather than a horrendous experience. I knew it would take time to see chemo the way she did, but I appreciated the door she opened for me. I knew that the worst I could ever do to myself would be to fight whatever treatment I agreed to. What it would take to accept and fully embrace the experience remained unknown, but I was willing to give it a try.

My Part

That quest of almost four months had been filled with lots of "us versus them" experiences. Everyone believed they had the answer, and each wanted me to go with them. "Pick me, pick me. Spend your time and money here. Trust me. I know what's best for you." It was like being at a carnival where each booth operator attempted to get me to "Come on over."

They didn't always say it out loud—sometimes it was inferred. At other times, some went so far as to say, "*They* don't know what they're doing or what they're talking about. They're only taking you further into harm's way." Sometimes the variation on the theme of how dangerous *they were* included, "What they're offering might not do you any more harm than waste your money, but why would you do that? Why would you waste your time, money, and energy?"

Looking back, I see how insane this process was—the world I entered of right versus wrong was pure crazy-making. And, as outrageous as the conventional practices of "cut, burn, poison" may have been, the world of "let us show you how right we are by demonstrating how wrong they are" was equally foolish—even selfish. As the person facing a life-threatening illness, the last thing I needed was to be involved in a battle between the two camps. They all thought they were coming from a place of caring and concern, and maybe they truly were, but what they left me with was more doubt, unease, distrust, and the inability to decide what to do next.

Thanks to Dr. David Simon and the entire Chopra Center team, I found my truth—the need to take an integrative approach to my treatment and, ultimately, my healing. This was such a "coming home" for me. Not being one who enjoys the battle, confrontation, or the need to choose who's right and who's wrong, I found peace in a decision that was right for me, peace in knowing I could take the best of both worlds and leave the rest. I could let go of what didn't fit. Not only did I find serenity in this knowledge, but freedom as well. I was able to listen within to all the counsel I'd received and then hear my own voice as it proclaimed exactly what would be best for me. And I could embrace the knowing that my ultimate healing would happen because I'd found my way, and there was no need to keep fighting the process.

Believe me, it wasn't easy. It took some time to view any potential treatment, as well as the surgery, as positive and beneficial. Yet, once I returned from the Chopra Center, I found I was no longer scattered. My out-of-control *Vata dosha* was no longer

110

out of balance. I didn't feel like I was being blown around by violent winds, unable to sit still, ground myself, or hear my deep inner knowing.

Before I left for the Chopra Center, I had been spinning in a frenzy of fear. *What do I do? Who do I believe? How can I find the right place, the right clinic, the right practitioner, the right elixir, the right healing modality? Who do I trust? What will be the perfect fit for me? What will cure me? And how long will it take?* Panicked, I'd almost chosen to spend tens of thousands of dollars *that we didn't have* at an out-of-state facility.

Within all this mental torment was my need to find the perfect solution—the guarantee that I would be well for years to come. I'd been so scared—scared of the cancer, scared of making the wrong choice, scared of the treatment, scared of the harm to my body, scared of weakening my body further, scared of dying, scared of living with cancer, scared of how cancer and my decisions would impact my life—that I'd become unable to move in any direction.

And I'd been so angry. *How did this happen to me? Why now? Why me?* Although I knew these questions were fruitless to dwell on, I couldn't seem to shake them. After trying so many modalities and practitioners, the thought that the cancer was still there and that it may have grown and spread was incomprehensible. I was angry at the people I'd put my faith and trust in and at myself for believing them—for *needing* to believe them.

Just prior to attending the Perfect Health program, I'd become frozen. I knew I needed to move forward, but I no longer trusted how to do that or who to listen to in order to decide. After my five days at the Chopra Center in Carlsbad, California, including many hours at the ocean, I'd found, for the first time in months, a sense of peace and calm within myself. I was still nervous, but I was no longer stuck.

Finally, I was ready to begin the process of once again taking action. But this time, it would be from a place of surrender rather than a place of fear. This time, it would be with the understanding that I could not control the *entire* process of returning to wholeness and health. My part would be to gather information to understand what would happen—the sequence, the when and how, and the how long. My part would be to gather all the wonderful positive energy that existed in my life through my family and friends. My part would be to add complementary modalities, such as massage and acupuncture and supplements, to support my treatment. My part would be to create guided imagery recordings and set up my "inner pharmacy," tapping into my senses of smell, touch, sight, sound, and taste—everything I'd learned about and connected to in those five days.

Then it would be time to surrender to the process of healing and wholeness through my Western doctors, my wellness team, and my family and friends, allowing each to help in my recovery. My part was to graciously accept what they offered. And most importantly, to release control of all the things I'd tried so desperately to hang on to, including my breast.

I've Made a Decision!

O n Sunday following my week at the Chopra Center,
as I drove back to LAX Airport, I called Dominic.
While I was away, I'd stopped calling home because
I found myself pulled into adolescent issues with our daughters,
as well as Dominic's fears about my health that he was struggling
to keep in check.

When he answered the phone, I took a deep breath and told
him I'd come to a decision. For a moment—silence. I knew he was
trying to brace himself for my next "new direction." I took another
big inhale and then blurted it out.

"I'm going to call the surgeon when I get home and schedule
my surgery," I said with as much courage and confidence as I could
muster. I instinctively knew he no longer had any idea what would
come out of my mouth.

"Okay?" he answered apprehensively.

I could tell he was dumbfounded and didn't know what to say in response. Over the next thirty minutes, I explained what had transpired and how I'd come to my decision. I admitted I was still scared, but I was ready to move forward. I then emphasized that I'd still bring in other healing to complement the surgery. I'd also do whatever the doctors said was necessary and accept whatever else I had to undergo to eradicate the cancer.

"Whatever you need to do, Donna, do it. I honestly thought you were going to tell me about another crazy scheme, and I was ready to tell you that I needed to leave for a while."

I hesitated for a moment. *Did I just hear him correctly?* I hoped I'd misunderstood since we were on speakerphone.

"You were going to leave?" I asked. I felt my heart drop to my stomach as my mouth went dry. A sense of panic started to fill the space where my heart had been.

"I just can't take any more experiments. I'm glad to hear you're finally willing to have surgery, though. I'll support you through it and take care of you. I'm just so relieved. It's time to get this out."

"But you were going to leave me? Leave the girls?" Tears began to build up behind my eyes. I tried to hold them back since I was driving on an LA freeway, and I needed to stay alert, but I felt like I'd just been sucker-punched in my gut. I could hardly breathe as I tried to take in what he was saying.

"For a while. To take a break. If you planned to keep going here and there and take more time to try new things, I knew I couldn't take the uncertainty anymore. So, I decided I'd take some time away. This has been stressful for all of us, not just you."

"But where were you going?" My questions had more to do with trying to wrap my mind around what he'd been contemplating rather than wanting to understand the logistics of his plan.

"I don't know. Greece … maybe to see my family for a while. I just knew I needed to get away from this if you were going to keep at it."

I felt crushed. It was clear I'd kept him in the dark and been chasing squirrels here, there, and everywhere, but he was actually going to leave me in the midst of my crisis? In my moment of need? I could feel my entire body begin to tremble. Up to this point, I'd counted on the fact that no matter what I did or how I acted, he'd be there. Apparently, that wasn't a given. I gripped the steering wheel to try and steady my shaking, sweaty hands.

"Well, I'm not," I answered, trying to swallow down my pride and hurt. "I know this has been hard for everyone, but I had to get to this decision in my way, in my time. I'm there … and I'm sorry it's impacted you and the girls. But I had no idea you would have left," I said as I tried to ignore the anguish that suddenly wanted to erupt. "I can't believe it, really."

"Well, I'm not leaving, and I wouldn't have left immediately or forever. I've just been so scared and stressed. I've felt helpless. It's been as if you haven't really needed me anyway."

It hurt to hear his words, but they were true. I hadn't wanted his help or his suggestions. I didn't want him to tell me what to do, when to do it, or with whom. I'd distanced myself so I could be the one in control of everything. Knowing he would have left hurt like hell, but was it really a surprise when I'd pretty much treated him like shit? I tried to stuff down my panic and sense of betrayal—to take a step back for a second and respond with words that acknowledged my behavior, even though his words still stung.

"I'll be home soon, and we can talk more. I'm sorry. I know this has been hard on everyone."

As I flew home, I thought about our conversation. I'd had no idea that he was ready to take time away from our marriage, but as hurt as I felt after hearing that, I knew why. I truly had spent a lot of time and money trying to find a way out, and I'd excluded him throughout my frantic search. From his perspective, as he watched his wife turning into an angry, controlling, even secretive woman, I must have sounded like a crazy zealot, manically darting from one idea, person, and treatment to another, all the while screaming about the horrors and injustices of Western medicine, the same Western medicine that had saved his life eleven years earlier. The same Western medicine that had saved our girls' lives. I had definitely put him and our daughters through hell, never giving them a second thought as I left the house for big chunks of time. I never tried to find out what he was thinking or feeling. But, as much as I wished I had behaved differently, I also knew I hadn't been able to deal with what was going on for him. I'd had no mental or emotional capacity for his thoughts and feelings.

Thankfully for all of us, I was ready to stop going off in different directions. My time chasing windmills was over. Now, I needed to suck it up and lick my wounds about what he'd been ready to do. He wasn't doing it. He said he was ready to support me, and I knew in my heart of hearts that he would. I hadn't wanted his help or support entirely before now. I'd wanted to believe I could handle everything myself. After nearly four months, I was finally ready to get the "prescribed" help that would remove the cancer. And I was ready to let him take care of me … at least a little.

Going It Alone

A s a child, I'd learned how to shut people out. For a while,
it was a coping mechanism I used with my parents. I did
it so well that at one point, my parents sought medical
help. Sometime during my elementary school years, my father decided I needed to be seen by our family doctor. He and my mom
were worried that I had a hearing problem.

For quite some time, I'd been unresponsive when they tried to
get my attention. They had to repeatedly say my name and eventually raise their voices before I acknowledged or seemed to be aware
they were talking to me. Because I suffered from frequent earaches,
they began to wonder if my hearing had been damaged.

The doctor performed simple tests, having me look away as he
made sounds that he asked me to respond to. He also had me listen
to the second hand on his watch and mark the rhythm with hand

gestures. Like a conductor keeping beat for an orchestra, I had to tick off the seconds with up and down strokes. I passed with flying colors. I seemed to have perfect hearing.

"So why can't she hear us when we call her or speak to her?" my dad asked.

"Well, I believe this is a case of selective hearing," our doctor replied, with the hint of a smile on his lips.

"What do you mean?" my dad queried, apparently not quite grasping the doctor's message.

"Well, Donna hears when and what she wants to hear," he explained. "It's called 'selective hearing.' If she wants to tune people out or wants to tune out sounds that bother her or sounds that interrupt her at times, she does. I believe that's what is going on here."

The doctor had figured it out. Sometime during my young life, I'd "learned" a way to block out sounds and live in my own internal world. It worked great for concentrating on schoolwork, and it became part of my survival mechanism when I didn't want to hear my parents arguing. Being extremely sensitive, I hated to hear them yell at each other, so I'd unconsciously found a way to tune out and check out.

I could now see how I handled my cancer journey prior to my time at the Chopra Center—alone and in my way, once again living in the internal landscape I'd created. I chose it that way. I hardly let anyone in—not friends, not my husband, not my daughters. I kept everyone at a distance that went way beyond arm's length and only told people, including my family, what I thought they needed to know. I did not give them a chance to let me know how they were feeling, to challenge me, or to make any waves. I especially didn't want to have to listen to them—I didn't want to hear what they had to say.

Although I was incapable of doing it differently at the time, I could see how difficult that had been for those who loved me, especially Dominic. I didn't want his opinions; I didn't want to know his fears. I could hardly handle my own. So, I kept him outside in that land of "need to know."

I went so far as to tell him, when he initially begged me to have a mastectomy, that he'd feel differently if it were his penis being considered. "You wouldn't let anyone cut that off!" I screamed. "So what makes you think I can so easily agree to have my breast lopped off? It may not seem like an essential part of my anatomy, but it is a huge piece of my identity!" I was ruthless in my analogy.

But how could I not be initially? Cancer could be ruthless too. And this was my life and my body. I got to decide, and I didn't want to be swayed by anyone—not even my daughters, and *especially* not him. He was the one to suggest we move to Colorado. Although I'd gone along with it, I still resented him for taking me away from everything and everyone I loved, and from everything and everyone our daughters loved. As much as I'd hoped we could all adjust to our new life, they were miserable, and deep down, so was I. I missed my family in California. I missed my friends. I missed the rolling hills and the Mediterranean climate. And I missed the ocean.

We'd spent my fiftieth birthday at the ocean at one of our favorite beaches, and it seemed that I likely wouldn't be spending future birthdays there. The ocean was my happy place; it had been since I was a child. It soothed me and reminded me of all the fun times I'd had in childhood there, including birthday parties, family vacations at the beach, bodysurfing and boogie boarding, and even sneaking away to spend time there as a teenager with the local surfers I idolized. Whenever I thought about what we'd left in California, I still found myself blaming him for taking me away from everything I loved. That made it easier for me to exclude him—blame and resentment served as a great justification for my behavior.

The bigger reason for excluding everyone, though, was not related to anger, resentment, or blame. It had everything to do with trying to find me. I chose to go it alone, at least for a while, so I could hear my own voice, listen to my heart, and feel my body. I had no capacity for anyone else's thoughts and feelings, and I sure didn't want their fears mirrored back at me. At all costs, I had to control whatever I could. Yes, I was ruthless, at least for a time, but sometimes drastic situations require drastic measures.

Amazon Woman

"You'll be an Amazon woman!" That's what one of my daughters said to me as we watched a television documentary about the Amazon women of ancient times. "You'll be just like them, Mom! They were strong and brave, and they didn't have their right breast either," she said excitedly as we both tried to make sense of what I had decided to do.

The legend goes that the Amazon women cut off their right breasts so they could aim their arrows and spears and send them exactly where they intended. They didn't want any potential interference that might cost them their people's food. They were responsible for the survival of their tribes, and feeding their people was more important than having a breast. They looked at the whole and considered the ALL in everything they did.

My eyes filled with tears. Could I get fully behind this decision that I'd struggled with for so many months? Could I see beyond my internal battle, which was now just an occasional skirmish, to what would be best for my family and my potential longevity? Was it possible for me to truly embrace being an Amazon woman?

Seeing my daughter's eyes filled with hope and pride and even relief, I knew she'd found my answer. *My eleven-year-old daughter is offering me a lifeline.* I could be defined by so much more than being a two-breasted woman or a victim of a disease that I'd feared since I was a girl. I could be strong and even beautiful. I truly had the ability to be an immensely powerful woman. It was time to consider the ALL of my life—to see the bigger picture. It was time to choose to live—to claim my place in the history of strong women who came before me. It was time to be an Amazon woman.

We're Not There Yet

On Monday, June 4, after returning from the Chopra Center, I called my surgeon. Coincidentally, she had an opening in her schedule for surgery the following Monday, June 11, due to a cancellation. I looked at my calendar and saw that it fell within the fourth quarter of the lunar cycle—one of my original requirements for surgery. I'd read that having surgery during the fourth quarter promotes faster healing and a better response to any surgical procedure. Along with her having an immediate opening, this was another sign to me that I was doing the right thing. Everything was falling into place, whether I was 100 percent ready or not. Again … there are no accidents.

I met with the surgeon that week, and she confirmed what Dr. Simon had said. "I doubt your lymph nodes have become involved. This is a slow-growing cancer. As I told you when you decided to wait, I didn't expect it to spread. Most likely, what the radiologist saw was the reaction of your lymph nodes trying to take care of the trauma from the biopsy. More than likely, they're doing what they're supposed to do—cleaning up the area—which makes them look more inflamed."

Although she couldn't know for certain until after the surgery, both doctors had now stated that they didn't think my lymph nodes were impacted. I could breathe a huge sigh of relief and do my best to take myself off the hook for not having decided sooner. It was obvious that I'd needed the time to look at other options. Otherwise, I might have always second-guessed my decisions. Now, at least my manic, frantic behavior, my ongoing quest for *another way*, could be put behind me. Although I still had mixed emotions and genuine apprehension, and although I was extremely sad to lose my breast, I finally knew I was doing the right thing.

I realized that instead of taking more actions, I now needed to sit with my feelings. To get myself mentally and emotionally prepared to undergo surgery, I needed to acknowledge the flood of emotions I felt—sadness, grief, anger, and disappointment that I hadn't found another way. I needed to do my best to be "all in" once the day of surgery came. No more doubting, no more fighting, no more struggle, no more striving. I had to surrender to my decision, to the surgeon I'd chosen, to being put under, and to having my breast removed.

On the eve of my surgery, I wrote in my journal:

"I don't hate my cancer. I just wish this had not happened. But maybe happening now does give me the opportunity to live the second half of my life differently. Maybe I can take more time for

125

myself—give me more of what nurtures me. Take more time to stop and smell the flowers. Take time to sing ... to dance ... to laugh ... to cry ... to lie in the sun. More time to give myself pleasure. I wish there was another way, but this seems to be the best thing I can do. And for now, I just have to accept the surgery—nothing else. I don't have to think about how I'll feel after the surgery because I'm not there yet. I don't have to think about the surgery so intensely today because I'm not there yet either. Today I still have my breast. I need to enjoy today and thank the cancer for what it has brought me ... new awareness ... new gratitude about life ... new ways of doing life. I will await the results of my pathology and I will *choose* what I will do from there. I will do what feels right and comfortable. Comfortable in the sense that I can live with what I do. I will wait for results without panicking about what is next. We're not there yet."

The Goodbye Ritual

I had wanted to do a ceremony—a ritual to say goodbye to my breast. I'd wanted to honor the part of my body that was an outward sign of my feminine self. But how?

All of my dearest friends were in California, and it wasn't possible for us to get together physically. I wasn't emotionally close enough to the friends I'd made in Colorado over the past year and a half for them to be part of such an intimate ceremony. No one in my current life would understand the ceremony I envisioned.

In the end, I resigned myself to the reality that I would hold no formal ritual of goodbye, no outward display of my inward sadness, as I let go of a part of me. I would have to silently and privately release my breast.

On the morning of surgery, I asked Dominic to take a photo of me bare-breasted so I would have an image to remember myself with two breasts. After he took a few photos, I asked for some time alone and stood in the bathroom with tears streaming down my face as I looked at my naked body. I knew that by evening, my image would never be this one. I was filled with deep sadness and grief for what I was about to lose, and I didn't know what to do with the emotions I was feeling.

Suddenly, I was in a different place and time. Our daughters were six months old. On that special day, in the midst of mowing the front lawn of our California home, Dominic came in and told me he was going to the ER because his chest was bothering him. He'd been complaining since the previous night about feeling a pain that went from the front of his body to his back. It had begun while he was changing one of the girls' diapers. Certain that he'd pulled a muscle from lifting both babies at the same time, I told him he was exaggerating and making a big deal about nothing. I couldn't understand why he needed to go to the ER and was angry at him, believing he was being a hypochondriac and ruining the Sunday half-year birthday we had planned with our girls. A few hours later, the house phone rang.

"I'm being admitted," he said immediately.

"What? Don't kid me like that," I answered in disbelief.

"I'm not kidding. They gave me nitroglycerin, and they're going to do an angiogram to see if there's a problem."

I could not believe he was actually being admitted to the hospital. That meant they thought there *was* a problem. Panicked, I called my parents and asked them to come right away. I needed help.

The following morning, I stood with the cardiologist who'd been called to the ER the previous day. As he played back the "movie" of Dominic's angiogram, he froze an image and pointed to a particular area.

"Based on his symptoms, I thought your husband might have a slight blockage that we could take care of with angioplasty. But … you see here … these areas … he's going to need bypass surgery because they are almost 100 percent occluded. I'm not a surgeon, but I believe he may need a quadruple or quintuple bypass. The surgeon will make that determination. I am so sorry to tell you this. I know he's a pilot and you have two infant daughters. I honestly can't believe that these blockages are so severe. He's only forty, he's thin, his cholesterol is not really high, and he presented as if he were almost asymptomatic. If he hadn't come in, though, I'm not sure how much longer he would have made it."

"Are you saying he could have died?"

"Well, with occlusions that are more than 90 percent, it could have turned into a life-and-death situation. Fortunately, he listened to his body—something few men do. Tomorrow, he'll be transferred and then scheduled for surgery. I am so very sorry, Mrs. Mazzitelli."

After I returned to the waiting room, I stepped outside with my best friend's husband. In shock and trying to make sense of what the cardiologist had just explained to me, I talked about what would happen next—on the following morning, Dominic would be transported to a hospital about thirty minutes away, where he'd be seen by the surgeon and scheduled for surgery.

"How will I manage this? How will I take care of the girls? I have to nurse them, and they need me. How will I go back and forth?"

"Well, you've nursed them for six months, which is more than a lot of women do. You'll need to stop nursing them and let your parents and us take care of them so you can be with Dominic."

Did he just say I needed to stop nursing? Why would I do that? Why would he say that? No! His words enraged me. No way would I stop nursing my babies at a time when their father's life was on the line. No one would or could tell me I had to stop nursing. I wouldn't choose convenience over their needs. They needed me. They were used to being fed by me—not with a bottle. And I desperately needed them. I needed some way to cling to life in the midst of the potentiality of death. My babies and I needed to hold on to each other through this ordeal. *Damn it! I will find a way!*

Three days later, after kissing Dominic goodbye as they wheeled him away to surgery, I sat in the waiting room with my parents, best friends, and my two babies, who lay in their double stroller. Through the hours of Dominic's surgery, I held my girls when they were awake, and I nursed them when they were hungry. Numb and afraid to think about what might happen once their father's chest was sawed and cracked open and he was put on a bypass machine for the surgery, I clung to them.

After learning that Dominic ultimately had quintuple bypass and that the riskiest part of the surgery had been when they switched him off bypass and waited for his heart to restart, I was grateful to the point of non-words for the fact that I'd had my girls to care for during a time when I could do nothing for Dominic but wait. My breasts had been a conduit of life-giving sustenance that nurtured me as much as them. They kept us all focused on life.

Later that night, when I was able to go in and see Dominic in recovery, I knew he wasn't yet out of the woods, but because he was only forty years old and in good health otherwise, he had a good chance of making it through. Prior to surgery, the surgeon had told us that Dominic most likely would never fly again, and Dominic and I had struggled with that information. I didn't know what would happen next for him or our family, and I was scared. Yet here he was, groggy but alive. As I approached his bed, I put on a brave face, leaned over, kissed his forehead, and told him he was going to be fine. We all would be.

With those memories, fresh tears rolled down my cheeks. I was back in my bathroom, looking at my bare-chested reflection in the mirror. I remembered all that had transpired after that post-surgical night. Juggling the care of our daughters with the needs of a husband who required help to do everything, including bathing and getting dressed; having my parents, my aunt, and other friends stay with us weekly to help out with the girls; attempting to pay our bills with no income coming in and feeling immense gratitude for the small checks and gestures that came by way of fellow pilots and flight attendants. Most of all, I recalled the overwhelm of not knowing how to help Dominic during his moments of frustration, anger, uncertainty, and despair. Amazingly, ten months later, Dominic regained his first-class medical and flew commercially once more. Through it all, I had continued to nurse my girls. Through the many ups and downs of his recovery and the process of regaining his medical, I was able to keep them close.

Because of those memories, I thought of our daughters. Our eleven-year-old girls were losing something too. Their first connection to life and trust in their own bodies. Not only were they watching their mother lose a breast, but they now knew that the multigenerational cancer was only one rung on the ladder away from them. Post-menopausal cancer had moved from my grandmother to my mother and now to me. They previously told me they were scared and angry—and they were sure that one day they'd have cancer too.

I thought more about their fear and anger. I couldn't promise them that they would never have breast cancer, but maybe I could help them consider that it could bypass them, or at the very least, that they could survive it. I needed to model that behavior rather than offer a sermon.

The anger they were feeling was a different story. There was an underlying energy around their anger that I hoped would dissipate one day—my daughters' anger at me. They felt betrayed by me, and I hoped we could mend what had been damaged—their belief that I was someone they could always and forever trust.

When I first learned I might have cancer, I didn't know the extent of it. Was it really cancer or a benign growth? If it was cancer, what stage and grade was it? Not having answers to those questions, I didn't want to tell the girls anything. I didn't want to alarm them if it turned out to be nothing. Yet, one night after taekwondo practice, when we stopped at our local vitamin and supplement store to pick up a cold remedy, the shop owner asked me how I was doing and if I'd found out whether or not I had cancer. I had gone to her immediately after being told I might have cancer so I could get some supplements to help boost my immune system and possibly eradicate any suspicious cells in my body.

The girls heard her question and looked at me in shock. "What?" they both asked. "What is she talking about?" they added before storming out to our car. I finished paying and let the shopkeeper know I hadn't yet shared anything with my girls. I followed them to our car and got in. In unison, they yelled at me and cried, "How could you? How could you keep this secret? You lied to us!" They were furious.

In Dominic's and my attempt to protect them, just as we'd done after 9/11, I could see that this time it hadn't been a good idea to keep information from them. They weren't six anymore, the age they were when their pilot father and I learned about the intentional and devastating plane crashes and decided to immediately shelter them from the fear that their father might die at the hands of another terrorist attack. They were now eleven—old enough to manage a fearful situation. At eleven, they needed to know the truth and not be left out. I immediately knew that by not telling them, we had unknowingly sent our daughters a message that they were incapable of handling the curveball life had thrown us. Keeping them in the dark and leaving them out of our family crisis sent them a message that they couldn't be trusted to navigate a difficult and scary time of uncertainty.

Admittedly, I had another motivation for my secret. Under the guise of trying to protect them, I'd also been doing it for me. In not telling them, I didn't have to try to support them and their feelings during a time when I could hardly acknowledge and manage my own. I was scared, not knowing if I had cancer or not, and I hadn't been ready to deal with their fear on top of mine. But as they cried and expressed their deep hurt, I could see that my need to protect myself in the name of protecting them was causing them even more pain. And I was left with an even bigger mess to navigate.

By the time we got home, they both told me they'd never forgive me for lying to them, for keeping the truth hidden from them. They went to their individual bedrooms and slammed the doors, leaving me with a clear message that what they were feeling went even deeper. The one person in their world they relied on to keep them stable and safe, the one who offered them hope, no matter what was happening in our family, had betrayed them. I had delivered a blow that shattered their world, destroying along with it every illusion of security and certainty they'd clung to, and they would never be the same.

So here I was, back in my bathroom, ready to go to the surgery center. In the months that had passed since that night in the car, life had stabilized, but I knew they still felt extremely hurt and betrayed. They'd kept a distance from everything I did during the months leading up to this moment, telling me they really didn't care. I knew they were still hurting, and I knew they were scared. Somehow, though, on this day, I felt I needed to include them in some way, at least to give them a chance to be a part of what would happen next. I wanted to begin taking steps back to living—and living beyond this diagnosis—and I wanted it to start immediately.

Suddenly, I knew what I had to do before Dominic and I left for the surgery center. It wouldn't be a big-ass ceremony or a well-orchestrated ritual. It would simply be a *moment*—a very private one—between three females who were bound together by blood and love.

I put on my bathrobe and called them into my bathroom, where we stood before the mirror.

"I am sad today because I have to lose my breast. But I am also grateful," I said. "These two breasts are part of what made me a woman, but not so much because of what men think of them. My breasts are much more than a part of me that brings pleasure to men. My breasts are more than a sexual symbol. My breasts fed you. They nursed you and comforted you. They were there when you needed soothing and calming. They provided a sense of safety and security to you. They did their job. And now, because I am grateful that they were able to care for you, I can say goodbye to the one and thank it for doing its job."

The girls looked at me as the next words came out of my mouth unexpectedly. "If you would like to thank my breast for feeding you and caring for you, you can give it a kiss or touch it like you did when you were young. You can thank it for the 'nana' it gave you. You don't have to, but if you want to say goodbye in that way, or in some other way, such as just saying 'thank you and goodbye,' you can. If you don't want to do or say anything at all, that's okay too. It's whatever you feel like doing or not doing."

They didn't say a word in response. For a moment, they stood there, looking back and forth at each other. Then, very slowly and silently, they exchanged looks with one another and separately walked up close to me, leaned in, and quickly kissed my breast. We continued to stand there in silence for another split second. Without saying anything more, they left the room. I knew they were feeling a mixture of eleven-year-old embarrassment for having come in contact with my breast but also gratitude for being acknowledged at a time when they felt scared and helpless. I turned back to the mirror as fresh tears slid down my face.

I'd had my ceremony after all. My ritual was complete. The only women who counted were there—my girls. They would know that we can live through this experience. They would know that we can still be whole and feminine and beautiful. And they would know that, above all else, our breasts were meant for our children.

I was ready. I had been blessed by the two people who mattered most to me in the whole world—my daughters. And as I went off to surgery, I was determined that this part of our family lineage would stop with me. If possible, this would be the end of the line for my family's post-menopausal breast cancer.

Nonessential Body Parts

When I was five years old, I underwent my first surgery—my tonsils and adenoids were removed. At the time, it was considered an essential surgery to eliminate reoccurring colds and ear infections. The parts removed, however, were thought to be unimportant. Unnecessary and nonessential to the body.

We now know that our tonsils and adenoids are part of our lymphatic system—with them removed, it seems that the rest of the lymph system has to work harder. The immune system is, in a sense, compromised. Tonsils and adenoids are rarely removed now.

My right breast was not considered to be an important part of the body either—the medical world doesn't seem to believe it is essential to a woman's life or her health. After all, the evidence appears to demonstrate that women can continue to live fully without a breast—even without both.

I wonder, though, if we will one day make a new discovery about this part of our anatomy. Will we one day determine that the breast plays a role beyond nursing our young or attracting men's attention like a flower attracts honeybees? Will we one day learn that our breasts, which reside in the area of our heart chakra, have a significant role in maintaining balance within the chakra system?

As humans continue to evolve, will we one day discover that the connection between heart and breast represents another system within our bodies that we have not yet identified, in the same way we know that our heart and lungs are part of our circulatory system?

Just as the ancient Egyptians believed that the heart was the center of our intellect, we, too, are learning that our heart is much more than a muscle that pumps and moves blood through our entire bodies. Our heart carries an intelligence that may be equal to or even surpasses that of our brain. Is it possible that our breasts, along with our heart, are the true source of intuition, wisdom, and even more? I wonder ...

Waking Up

After my tonsils were removed, I woke up with a terrible sore throat that made it extremely painful to swallow. I cried, which only made the pain worsen. The nurses tried to coax me with ice cream and Jell-O, assuring me that the cold would soothe the intense discomfort I was feeling. I was afraid to put anything in my mouth—especially afraid to let anything go down my throat. I thought it would make me feel worse. I didn't trust what the nurses were telling me, and I was scared. For the first day, I refused.

When I awoke from my mastectomy, I felt no physical pain. I was even somewhat euphoric in those initial moments, knowing I was on the other side of a decision that had taken so long and been so hard to come to. I'm sure the pain meds were helping.

As I lay there, I began to orient myself to my surroundings. The more awake I became, the more clearly I understood that my surgery was over—it was done, and my breast was gone. It took a while to let that knowing sink in. Lying on my back, I attempted to look down at my chest and saw the bandaging wrapped snuggly around my upper body. I couldn't see anything beyond the gauze. I couldn't feel anything either, at least not on the outside. Even on the inside, in those initial moments, I felt only numbness.

Beyond that, though, as my awareness came into fuller focus, I sensed something else. Deep within—way beyond the bandages and the incision—was a pain that would not be coaxed away or soothed by something cold and sweet. Soft words of comfort wouldn't be able to eliminate the realization and accompanying sorrow that began to surface. I was now a one-breasted woman— an Amazon. A part of my feminine identity was gone. A part of me that had nursed my girls was no more.

How will I soothe away this ache that goes to my core? Is there a food or salve that can relieve this kind of pain? Or will time and gentleness and patience need to be my guides?

Once I got home from the hospital after my tonsillectomy, I quickly forgot about my tonsils. The pain in my throat went away, and I was able to eat whatever I wanted. Once the physical pain was gone, so, too, were all the memories of having my tonsils removed. I knew my breast would be a different experience.

Dismantled

What happens to a breast after they dismantle it,
after they dissect it and pick it apart?
Does it end up in biohazard waste?
How did my breast become trash—
disintegrated and disposed of in a red plastic bag?
The same breast that was once considered beautiful.
The breast that not so many years earlier nurtured and nourished.
How did it become something to be analyzed and feared,
to be shredded and pulpified and discarded?

*How did it change from a symbol of life
to an object of potential death?*

Where did my breast go?
I'll never know the answer to that question.
I can only hope wherever it ended up, it is at peace.

A Mixture of Emotions

Week one post-surgery was a mixture of numbness, sadness, regret, guilt, and relief. My breast was gone, but so was my cancer. Based on the path of the Steri-Strips across my chest, it seemed I would be left with a scar much longer than I'd anticipated. I cried as I realized the scar wouldn't look anything like the cute sketch the surgeon had shown me in her book. Because of that drawing, I'd expected it to be a short, pretty little crescent shape rather than the obvious straight line that extended at a slight diagonal beyond where my breast had been—the strips went from under my armpit to the center of my chest.

Having been told the Steri-Strips would fall off over the next couple of weeks, I wondered whether or not I would be able to accept my new body and come to terms with becoming Amazon Woman. As much as this new version of me would take time to process, I tried to console myself by remembering that Amazon Woman was destined for a long life. At this early stage in my healing, however, that didn't work so well.

Within a few days, a new awareness entered my mind, and it had the potential to take me into the darkness of self-hatred. I began to question my decision. *Did I do the right thing? Should I have tried another treatment before succumbing to surgery? Could I have had a lumpectomy instead?* No matter the questions, and no matter my musings, I always came back to the same place: *Yes, I did the right thing and I did it at the right time. I need to stop tormenting myself with self-doubt.*

Then another thought began to plague me. I looked at my left breast. My nipple pointed away from center, toward my left upper arm, and at a downward angle since my breast was beginning to sag with age. I wondered if I should have had my left breast removed as well because it wasn't *very pretty.* Then, almost feeling disgust at the look of my healthy breast, I started thinking it should have been the one that needed to go. Disgust turned to guilt for allowing such thoughts, chastising myself for rejecting my remaining breast. I felt ashamed that I was letting such crazy thoughts infiltrate my mind. I knew I hadn't wanted to remove my healthy breast prophylactically, so why was I now criticizing it, almost wishing it gone? *I need to trust that I did the right thing,* I told myself. *I need to love my body and all its remaining parts.*

It was apparent that I'd been given the way out of my four-month ordeal. Once I'd been shown the *right* course of action, I'd been given the opportunity to act quickly on my decision to have surgery. *It's time to love my remaining breast and grieve the one*

I lost. I need to believe that my desire to live a long, healthy life is being supported—and that it has been all along. I tried to talk my way back to trust and faith in my decisions.

Week two post-op was shrouded in a sense of melancholy and subdued feelings. I couldn't seem to shake depression. In the midst of such deep-seated sadness, I recognized that I almost always carry an aura of melancholy. Where it comes from and why, I couldn't explain. Others see me—and most of the time I see myself—as an optimist and a positive thinker. But just under the surface runs emotion that I rarely let up and out. It feels attached to a sense of doom and gloom and has to do with me not really being loved or loveable. Although the physical disease had been removed, I began to acknowledge that I had work to do to remove the mental disease that lived deep within.

During those first two weeks, I also had many disturbing dreams. Dreams of murder and torture. Dreams of people being killed with machine guns. Violent dreams. Frightening dreams. Dreams of being told by my surgeon and oncologist that I needed to undergo chemotherapy. A dream of shame as a man pursued me sexually and I realized I only had one breast. I froze. How could I let him see me? In my dream, I knew my body wasn't beautiful anymore. Then came a dream that left me feeling extremely sad. Women were walking around bare-breasted at a place that seemed to be an oceanside spa resort. I said to someone, "I'll never be able to do that ... to bare my breasts again." In the midst of the dream, I felt shame and embarrassment as well as sadness. When I awoke, I wondered when I'd be able to say, "This is who I am, this is how I look, and I'm proud to be alive and healthy!"

It began to sink in that I would never look how I looked before surgery. I would carry this very large scar until I died. I could choose to have it serve as a reminder that I must never forget to take care of myself, to nurture myself, to speak up for myself, and to not carry the burdens of others. It could also serve to remind me that above all else, I chose life. I wanted to live and was given that gift. But holding on to such thoughts would take time.

Once the pathology report came back and confirmed that the cancer had not spread to other areas and that it had involved a few small areas of my breast, I started to wonder once again if the surgery had been necessary. But every time I revisited the self-doubt that wouldn't seem to go away—and the telephone conversation with my surgeon, who reassured me that because of where the cancer had been, I wouldn't have been a candidate for a lumpectomy after all—I knew a mastectomy had been the right choice. The surgery took away all traces of the localized cancer, and I would not have to go through any follow-up radiation or chemotherapy treatments.

My journal has always been the place where I can get honest. In the early morning hours, when the house is quiet and no one else is yet awake, I can sit and write from a place of deep reflection. Sometimes, the truth eludes me as I wallow in self-pity or vent about how I've been wronged and by whom, but at some point, oftentimes during the same journaling "session," I get to the core truth of whatever is going on. Sometimes I get insights about the "real truth" and my part in it, as well as a clear sense of how to move forward.

My journal is where I can bear my deepest thoughts and feelings and allow them to be revealed. I do my best not to judge or deny what pours out onto the page, but I sometimes find myself as both the participant and the observer in the writing process.

At times, the observer becomes the inner critic, telling me what I should do and when I need to do it, and even that it's time to get over myself. At other times, the observer becomes the compassionate one, allowing me to be exactly where I am, holding space for my angst and pain. And then there are those times when the observer is so far in the background that I hardly know she's there. Whenever I'm aware of her presence, I do my best to thank her for being there and try not to let her influence what flows out of me. No matter how she shows up, though, I do at least acknowledge her perspective.

In the subsequent weeks after my surgery, as I struggled to re-engage with life, I did a lot of journaling. I'd been on a mission for so long to rid myself of cancer that now I couldn't seem to find my purpose and focus. It was easy to focus on nutrition and supplements and spiritual practices when I was in the midst of the crisis, but now maintaining discipline seemed challenging, especially since I was having difficulty connecting with life and living. I journaled about lots of "shoulds," but feeling fully alive seemed elusive. "I really do want to live cancer-free," I wrote. "I don't want to live chasing the cancer. And I don't want to live in a way that I feel bound to my disease. But how do I do that?"

Eventually, as I continued to reflect in the pages of my journal, my observer-self showed up as the compassionate one, and I welcomed her. At that point, I truly needed her to weigh in. I was able to tell myself that this process could not be rushed. It would take whatever amount of time it took to feel whole again, to engage with living rather than being stuck in fear that I would die, or to let go of regret and grief for what I lost. It would also take time to see what I'd experienced as a blessing. When this would happen and what it would take for me to get there remained a mystery. In the meantime, I needed to stop "shoulding" on myself.

Is It Vanity?

"**M**onday—1st week." That's what the outside of the beautifully hand-designed envelope read. It had been sent on the day of my surgery. Inside was a card from one of Louise Hay's affirmation decks, and the front of the card's message was: "I release all fears and doubts." The back of the card was filled with three additional affirmations: "I am loved and I am safe. I now choose to free myself from all destructive fears and doubts. I accept myself and create peace in my mind and heart."

The card had been sent by one of my girlfriends in California, a woman I adored and with whom I'd become close during the six years we homeschooled our children together. Our daughters were the same age, and we had been involved in many activities together, including a small science and nature co-op and weekly ice skating lessons.

Long before that card arrived, she and I had had a tough conversation, one in which she questioned my motives for not immediately having surgery. At the time of our conversation, I told her I wasn't sure I could go through with it and was looking at other options. She initially thought it was because I wanted to remain a two-breasted woman—no matter the cost.

She told me about a woman in her twenties who had recently been diagnosed with breast cancer. The woman was understandably devastated. She was large-breasted and appreciated how she looked. She was also single and dating. How could she go through such a disfigurement? She'd decided not to undergo surgery at the time, which doctors were strongly recommending. Instead, she was going to try alternative methods first.

In so many ways, I understood this young woman's dilemma. I didn't know what kind of cancer they'd found or what her prognosis was, but I did understand how it might feel to have to undergo such a big physical change, even having to come to terms with a cancer diagnosis in her twenties. My girlfriend was concerned that this woman was risking her life in the name of "vanity." It made her question why I was stalling. And just like so many others who loved me, she was worried that my delays could have detrimental consequences.

Is it vanity? I had asked myself at the time. Well, to begin with, I was rather small-breasted. I didn't even have cleavage. My breasts were definitely not my best or my favorite feature. My breasts didn't look beautiful to me, so I didn't think it was about vanity.

Initially, I was angry that lumpectomies and mastectomies seemed almost like casual decisions from the perspective of the medical community—decisions that physicians seemed to expect patients to make without much thought other than which procedure was most appropriate. Although breast cancer has become rather "common," and mastectomies are often elected by women rather than lumpectomies (sometimes even electing to simultaneously remove the second "healthy" breast), the decisions are still extremely personal. As a woman needing to make such a decision, I wanted to be seen and treated as an individual. And I wanted to be graced with time to come to the right decision for me. Was it vanity? I didn't think so. Was it self-focused and even self-absorbed? Yes, most definitely.

If I held a piece of sadness and fear related to my looks, it was in wondering how I would be able to accept myself as a one-breasted woman—how would I ever begin to feel "whole"? And I wondered if Dominic would still find me attractive or be repulsed by me.

Thinking more about it, I had never loved my body. This was a deep-seated, lifelong truth. For as long as I could remember, I only saw my body's flaws: cellulite, thick thighs, big belly. Many months after I gave birth to my twins, one of my neighbors asked me if I was pregnant again. This was the second time in my life I'd been mistaken for carrying a child. Finding out that I wasn't, she offered suggestions for exercises to tighten up my belly. I'd struggled with my weight since I was a teenager. Never obese, but there were times when I was at least twenty pounds overweight, so I constantly considered my body defective. It embarrassed me, and I was ashamed of it more than I ever loved it.

But at fifty-one, I'd begun to accept it. My fluctuating weight was a problem of the long-ago past because I began to focus less on dieting and instead concentrated on eating habits as a lifestyle. I still had flab and cellulite, which still embarrassed me, but I didn't focus on it as much—only when I had to put on a bathing suit. And I rarely paraded around naked.

Then what did losing my breast really signify? The answer: another flaw. Confirmation that I hadn't taken care of myself as well as I could and should have—that maybe I could have eaten even better and maybe I could have dealt with life's challenges in an emotionally healthier way. Losing my breast represented another huge imperfection. A sudden change to my body that would be a challenge to accept. Was it connected to vanity? I still couldn't say for certain. More than anything, it related to another reason not to love and accept who I was. It went deeper than my looks.

As my friend and I talked longer, she softened. She heard my pain and my fear. She listened to my anger and frustration. She opened to my grief. She understood my struggle to accept myself no matter what. She said she'd support me in whatever I decided to do, and she did.

We stayed in touch by phone during the months before I decided to have surgery. When I finally did undergo my mastectomy, her cards began to arrive in place of our phone calls. She knew I would need time to process what I'd been through, so for about three weeks, her beautiful cards appeared in my mail—each day with a different affirmation that she had chosen especially for me, contained in a specially designed, handcrafted envelope that she had created just for me. Sometimes, she even affixed homemade stickers to the envelopes with more special messages meant just for me.

These cards and the envelopes they came in filled me with her love and an open invitation to learn to love and accept myself—all of me. One of the last cards to arrive contained this message: "I trust the process of Life. There is a rhythm and flow to Life, and I am a part of it. Life supports me and brings to me only good and positive experiences. I trust the process of Life to bring me my highest good." Oh, how I wanted this to be true and for me to believe it with every fiber of my being. I knew I had a long way yet to go, but I was determined to get there.

I still have those cards and envelopes in my bedside table and look at them any time I need a dose of belief, trust, and self-love. A gift that will be available to me for as long as I live.

Swimming

In the days following surgery, most of the back of my arm to my elbow and the front of my arm down to my fingers, especially my ring finger and little finger, were numb and tingly. The tingling traveled to my back, all the way to my shoulder blade. I worried whether the upper right side of my body was okay. *How much nerve damage will I be left with?* Between the potential for permanent lymphedema and possible permanent nerve loss, I hoped my surgeon had been as good as everyone said she was.

The numbness and tingling continued, and when I shaved under my arms, I had to be extra careful on my right side and watch what I was doing as I applied the razor to my skin. I couldn't feel anything at my armpit—not even the slightest sense of pressure—so I had to use my eyes to determine how much pressure to apply and how to move the razor. As the days passed, I wondered if I could do anything to help myself regain more feeling.

"Why don't you start swimming as soon as the surgeon says you can get into a pool?" Dominic asked. "You've always loved to swim!"

He was right. Swimming had always brought me pleasure. It was an experience of pure joy whenever I had the chance to be submerged in water. From the time I was a little girl, I loved whenever I got to be in a pool. Even in high school, I competed for a while. I had a mean sidestroke and enjoyed synchronized swimming. Thinking about strokes like the crawl and the breaststroke, I imagined my chest being able to expand and stretch. Maybe by increasing my range of motion, I could help bring life back to my nerve endings. I also thought about being supported by the surrounding water. It was as if I entered a watery cocoon when I got into a tub or pool of water—a place that felt safe and far away from landlocked issues that made me feel anxious or afraid. The more I thought about it, swimming did seem to be the answer.

Except for one problem. The idea of swimming was easier to entertain than the reality of doing it. To swim, I would have to put on my bathing suit, a suit that was made for the two-breasted version of me. How would I pull it off when I wouldn't have a prosthetic for a while longer? I definitely couldn't stuff my bathing suit with tissues!

Soon after, I got up the nerve to try on my bathing suit. As I slipped my right arm and then my left arm in, I was scared to straighten up and look in the mirror. I anticipated looking at a bathing suit that went inward at the site where my right breast had been. How surprised I was to find that both built-in cups curved outward, making it look as if nothing had changed. *Could I pull it off?*

At three weeks post-op and now permitted to fully submerge in water, I got up enough nerve to take myself to one of our community pools. As I placed my towel on the grass, I considered what I would do next. *I'll sit here for a little while and warm up. Then I'll take off my cover-up and soak up the sun for a bit longer. Then I'll nonchalantly stand up and walk over to the edge of the lap lane area. I'll slip into the pool and check to see how my chest looks as I submerge myself into the water. Then I'll start to slowly do some laps. When I am ready for a break, I'll start to raise myself on the ladder and double-check my chest area. If I need to adjust the cup, I'll slide back into the water, push the cup outward from inside my bathing suit with my left hand, then I'll get out and walk casually over to my towel. That should work without anyone noticing anything.* I had my plan and was ready to give it a try.

I felt my anxiety increase as I raised my cover-up over my head. Checking that my bathing suit still poked outward at my chest, I leaned back on my towel and took deep breaths. "You can do this. You can," I told myself. Once I started to feel hot from the sun's rays, I stood up and walked over to the pool as casually as I could, although my legs were quivering. I took more deep breaths. "You can do this," I repeated to myself. I slipped into the water and immediately looked downward. The cups of my suit were floating outward! I was amazed and relieved and started to relax a little. "It's time," I whispered. "You've got this. Swim!"

I started out ever so slowly doing a front breaststroke, keeping my arms close to my sides. With each stroke, I let my arms go a little bit wider, allowing the stiffness on my right side to release, yet careful to not overextend and cause myself unnecessary pain. After a lap, my arms were almost completely extended. I smiled inside. *You can do this! You've got this. Keep swimming!* After another lap, I was fully extended. I decided to try a sidestroke, lying on my left side. It would allow me to keep my right arm close to my body. *You're doing it!* I thought to myself. *You're swimming!*

After a few more laps, I felt tired. Good tired. The kind of tired associated with physical accomplishment. I was ready to get out and take a break. *Okay,* I coached myself. *Do it just as you visualized.* I swam over to the ladder and put my right leg on the first rung. With the second rung, my chest was just above the water. I looked down. The cups of my suit were still poking outward. *No need to adjust anything.* I raised myself up and stepped out of the pool. As I made my way to my towel, I felt the release of endorphins. *You did it! You did it! You swam!* Ecstatic and relieved, I lowered myself onto my towel, lay back, and stretched out, letting the sun's warmth penetrate my body.

The following day, I wrote in my journal: "I did something very brave yesterday, and it felt so good! I went swimming and wore my bathing suit to the pool. I almost felt normal—some of the time, I did feel normal. At times, I forgot I only had one breast. Then there were times when the pain came back—like when I tried to raise my arms as I lay down and I remembered that I needed to be careful with my movements, or when I tried to lay on my stomach and I hit the lump on my chest left by the drain that had been there after surgery." As with all mastectomies, a tube had been left in my chest post-operatively to make sure excess fluids could drain out rather than accumulate and cause internal issues post-surgically.

My journal entry continued: "I swam and it felt good—I went slowly as I extended my arms, but I was able to do the breaststroke and sidestroke. I didn't try the crawl, but I will. I felt so proud of what I was able to do. When I got out of the pool, I suddenly thought about what I must look like. Yet, I was okay. The cups in my bathing suit made it look like there were two small breasts inside. The visual worked, and it was freeing. Yesterday, I took my first steps back to living! Soaking up the sun also felt good. I am alive, and I'm going to live!"

For weeks, I'd been struggling to accept the physical change to my body. As the Steri-Strips began to fall away and the dark purple scar and pucker under my arm became more exposed, my sadness, grief, and shame had grown. Styling my hair one morning, the profile of my right side reflected back at me from the full-length mirror on the side wall. The image caught me by surprise—from that angle, I looked like a pre-pubescent girl. Having to acknowledge the loss of my nipple and my new flat-chested profile was difficult to take in. Yet, swimming gave me a gift I hadn't expected. Being immersed in water and physically exerting my body as I moved from one end of the pool to the other had more to do with what my body was capable of rather than how it looked. My body felt good when I swam—it felt powerful and strong. As my range of motion increased, so did my confidence in my body's ability to do everything it had been able to do before surgery. Acceptance of how I looked might not come easily, but swimming would help me feel my strength and come to appreciate this new version of me—a truly brave Amazon woman.

Where Are We Now?

About a month post-op, our closest friends from California came for a visit to celebrate my fifty-second birthday. They had been the ones I called in the middle of the night when I was freaking out about my diagnosis and possible prognosis. They had been at our side at crisis points in our lives, including the premature birth of our girls and Dominic's bypass surgery. Close friends who were there for us through it all. However, because we had moved to Colorado, the four of us had not been together in a long time, and they wanted to come and celebrate my good news with us—that there would be no further need for treatment of any kind. My cancer was gone!

Denise had been studying with a mosaic artist and creating her own pieces for a while, so packed in her luggage, weighing at least twenty pounds, was a special gift—a round mosaic "stepping stone" she had created especially for me.

It depicted the sun and its rays, surrounded by a brilliant blue sky. At the center of the circular stone, the broken, irregular tiles formed a bright yellow circle with orange rays that shot out to the ends of the stone. In between the orange rays, the sky was represented by various shades of blue ceramic pieces. In one section of the sky, an iridescent blue "gem" shone—a reminder that no matter what, we are each a beautiful gem, even when we feel broken.

After they settled in our guest room, Denise presented me with this incredible reminder of my light and of strength and hope. I was filled with gratitude and awe for what she had created, especially for me. We placed it at the center of our patio table, where it remains a centerpiece of our backyard.

It was wonderful to be able to celebrate life and living with them and to show them some of the nearby places we love. One of those places was Estes Park, about two hours away from our home. We took them to this quaint mountain town to enjoy lunch and a leisurely walk through the local shops. As much as I wanted to truly enjoy this time with them, I soon discovered that even though my cancer was gone, much in my life was damaged, including my relationships with food and Dominic.

We found a restaurant that served simple American fare, including hamburgers, fries, and salads—our daughters' favorite foods at the time. Since I'd made a commitment to change my diet after I was diagnosed, I'd stopped eating meat, dairy, processed white flour, white sugar, and I'd stopped drinking coffee. Looking over the menu, I could not find one item that didn't include at least one of these "bad" foods—dangerous foods in my mind. I became agitated and angry as I struggled to find a menu item that

I could feel comfortable eating. On top of that was the issue that at home, I only ate organic foods. Absolutely nothing on this menu was organic.

Seeing how upset I'd become, everyone offered that we could go to a different restaurant. In a petulant tone, I told them, "No. I'll figure out something. There is no need for us to go somewhere else."

It was the weekend, and Estes was busy. Going anywhere else would mean a wait, and our group was hungry. Besides, the girls really wanted to have hamburgers. I knew I was acting childish, but I couldn't seem to help it. Trying to rein in my behavior, I told myself to suck it up and make a decision.

I asked to order last, and by the time the server got to me, I opted for a small green salad with oil and vinegar that I could put on myself. I told her to hold the cheese. When my salad arrived, I saw that it was sprinkled with cheddar cheese. I was furious but didn't say a word to the server—I didn't want to delay our meal by having them remake my salad. I'm sure my family and our friends were uncomfortable, though, as I complained about the restaurant's faux pas after our server left, but no one said a word. By then, everyone knew I was inconsolable. It turned out that even the oil tasted rancid. Knowing that this was supposed to be a time for us to enjoy being together, I shut my mouth and attempted to eat, picking out the cheese with my fingers and wiping the pieces onto the extra paper napkin I grabbed and placed at the side of my plate.

When we left the restaurant, we decided to stroll along the main street and browse the many shops. Everyone was more than ready to shift the energy. Our girls took off separately to be on their own for a while. At one point, Denise and Dave were ahead of us, walking hand in hand. I looked at Dominic, who was walking beside me, and took in the distance between us.

"We never hold hands anymore," I commented, suddenly aware of just how far apart we'd drifted. Without a response, Dominic continued to walk. Neither of us made any attempt to rectify the situation. I tried to convey that we needed to start touching each other again, including holding hands, but neither of us seemed to know how to begin. The chasm between us was obviously much bigger than we had been willing to acknowledge. As we continued to walk, I hoped our friends hadn't noticed just how far apart Dominic and I had grown. And I wondered if we would ever make it back from this abyss.

It would take years to find our way back to each other. We didn't know it on this day, but we both needed to address our own fears, our own sadness and grief, and even our regrets about what we'd lived through during the past four years. Alone and separate from each other, we would need to consider everything that had happened to us and our family since the time Dominic lost his medical clearance to fly four years earlier. We would each need to come to terms with the decisions we'd made and all that had transpired from that point, including our move to Colorado. Our journey forward would require self-reflection, self-compassion, self-forgiveness, and the passage of time to understand that what we had chosen to do had all been done with intentions based on love for each other, our children, and yes, even ourselves. On this day, however, all we knew was how incredibly far apart we had grown.

A Black Belt Says It All

Triumph ... perseverance ... commitment ... strength ... courage ... tenacity ... humility ... gratitude. These words reflected the journey forward post-surgery.

I was cancer-free and on my way to becoming stronger in mind and body. Two weeks post-op, shortly after the chest tube had been removed, I tested for my taekwondo red belt, flanked by my daughters as they went through the moves of my form with me. I felt their love, support, and encouragement as I attempted to remember and execute each move with precision and confidence.

It was a triumphant moment when the head instructor and owner of the school handed me my belt, just two away from the black belt I was training to achieve. Accomplishing this so soon after my surgery, I was certain I'd be able to move forward and catch up to earn my black belt side by side with my daughters.

Fourteen months later, I stood alone on the mats of the dojo to perform my solo form that I had created and set to music, one of the requirements to earn my black belt. I'd had many starts and stops the previous year, experiencing emotional ups and downs that made me realize I wasn't ready to move forward. Months earlier, I had pulled back from testing because I knew I didn't have the mental attitude or deep conviction to see it through. I had to let go of the idea that I'd test alongside my daughters.

It was humbling to admit that I wasn't ready to do it—that I just couldn't. I was still healing emotionally and didn't have the mental capacity to remember everything I'd be required to demonstrate. My passion, determination, and drive were at an all-time low.

As time passed, though, I became stronger physically and mentally. Finally, I was ready to put my skills to the test. On a warm August night, I stood before a panel of six judges, most of whom I'd become acquainted with over the past two and a half years. I felt mentally sharp and physically strong. I knew I was ready.

The music began, and Melissa Etheridge sang out two verses and the chorus of "I Run for Life" while I executed the blocks, strikes, kicks, and moves with my long staff. I knew every move intimately, and Melissa and I were one in that moment, both having come through an experience with breast cancer. Around me, tears flowed, even from some of the male judges. Melissa's song and my choreographed form told a story of hope and triumph.

I had done it—lived through a difficult time, found my voice in the process, and chose decisions that were right for me. Just as the form I now performed was mine alone, so had my experience of cancer been exclusively mine.

Each choice I made, every action I took, was what I decided would serve me best. In the end, they had been the right ones, executed by the best people to support me. On this night, as my black belt was tied around my waist by one of the judges, tears flowed down my cheeks.

I was a woman like no other—strong, vibrantly alive, energetic, enthusiastic, and grateful. I had been to a dark place but now stood here as an Amazon woman, ready to continue living life to the fullest with the knowing that if I have myself—all of me—then anything is possible. It wasn't a breast that made me complete—it was a belief in myself and the connection to my mind, body, and essence that made me whole. From that wholeness, everything is possible. Health … longevity … love … healing … even a black belt!

I stand in front of the mirror
One breast stares back at me.
"You'll be an Amazon woman," my daughter said.
I don't need to draw a bow or thrust a spear into the air.
I had to excise the uninvited inhabitant.
Not a warrior in this lifetime.
Only a peaceful single-breasted woman
Who has to learn to love herself
No matter what.

A Women's Healing Circle

A *healing group. Not a support group. I want to create a healing group.* These were the thoughts that entered my mind once I was healed physically. I wanted a return to other ways of supporting perfect health, and I wanted to do it in community. Whatever I chose to create, I wanted it to feel spiritual, but more than anything, I wanted it to support me and other women in eating clean and healthy, in taking care of our bodies physically, and in supporting us psychologically and emotionally after having gone through such a challenging time. I wanted to form a group that did more than support cancer walks and cancer fundraisers. In fact, I wanted the focus on health and healing rather than on cancer and treatment. I wanted to bring a group of women together to sit in circle and find our way to stronger immune systems and genuine joy-filled lives.

Through people I'd been working with to support my continued healing, I connected with a few other women and, soon enough, we were meeting on prescheduled Saturdays. I brought in guests to talk to us—including an acupuncturist, a compounding pharmacist, and energy healers. We also read books like *The China Study* to learn more about what we ate. We learned about supplements to support us, and we talked about the experiences we'd been through medically. A few of the first members were going through reconstructive surgery, so they were able to talk about what that process was like for each of them. I didn't want this group to become a cancer support group, but I knew that in order to support healing, we had to tell our stories of what we'd been through and what we were still dealing with.

Initially, there were four of us, but after more than six months, other women began to join us on occasion. When that happened, the conversations reverted to a focus on treatment modalities, as these women were still undergoing treatment, and they were suffering. We also began to occasionally cancel meetings because enough of our core group couldn't meet due to outside conflicts. It seemed that the needs of the group were changing.

As the core members felt more confident about themselves—how they were feeling physically and what life changes they'd made—they seemed to need the group less. And when we did meet, because of new attendees' needs, the conversation began to refocus on chemo and its effects and reconstructive surgery and all it entailed. Our group no longer felt like the evolving healing circle as we'd started out. I also had to admit to myself that I couldn't relate to the conversations taking place because I hadn't undergone post-surgical treatment or reconstruction. I started to feel like an impostor and "less than" in my own group, which I'd never felt when we began.

I knew I was grateful I hadn't undergone what these women were experiencing, but when new members joined us and we went around the room to introduce ourselves, my language began to shift as I described my experience. I heard myself using "just" and "only" when I talked about my journey with cancer. "I *just* had a mastectomy. Fortunately, I didn't have to go through chemo or radiation. I *only* had to have surgery." It almost felt like an apology, like my experience was less than theirs, and I had to be sorry for that. It felt like I wasn't truly an Amazon woman because what I'd experienced wasn't as intense and didn't last as long as their treatments.

Of course, no one expressed these thoughts, and my use of "just" and "only" was always followed by, "Oh how lucky for you," or "Wow, how fortunate you were." Their words were sincere, yet that's not how I felt. I was still dealing with residual physical issues, especially numbness, and I was still working on accepting how I looked. I'd opted not to undergo reconstructive surgery because I didn't want to further tax my immune system. Instead, I wanted to rebuild it, as well as my confidence in my body that I initially felt had betrayed me. These were a large part of my reasons for starting the healing circle—so we as women could heal internally and externally. But increasingly, I didn't feel I had a right to express what was going on for me.

When I started the healing circle, even though my experience was different from the others, I felt valuable, even "equal." I'd gathered

169

so much alternative and integrative information and connected with so many other practitioners that I felt what I was bringing to our core group more than qualified me to be a "member." And as we tried new things together, including new foods and recipes, what we were sharing was as helpful and supportive to me as it was to them. Yet, when new women joined us who were in the throes of treatment, they had no mental, physical, or emotional capacity for what our core group was doing. I began to feel inadequate in what I could offer and in how I could or could not relate to their experiences.

I could see that we either had to adjust to the changing needs or let go of our group. After discussing it with our core group, we ultimately decided to disband. The others didn't want to become a cancer support group either—they'd never wanted that. As we talked about our journey over the previous year and a half, we acknowledged how much we'd all benefited from our group. We'd learned a lot from our reading and from our guests. We'd all adjusted our lifestyles to support our health and a "return to wholeness." We were healing more and more internally as well, feeling less and less fear about what had happened to us. We were all committed to living in healthier, life-affirming ways. It was a good decision for all of us. We were ready to move forward.

Afterward, though, I continued to think about what had been going on for me internally. Why did I get to the point where I felt my experience didn't qualify me? Why did I minimize what I'd been through? Others in the group had aggressive forms of cancer, while mine had been non-aggressive—why did I think that made my cancer less significant than theirs? When I really looked at it, I could see that almost from the beginning of our healing circle, I thought I didn't have a right to feel anger or sadness—especially because I had been one of the *luckier ones*. Why had I begun to feel "less than" the others?

This was an old pattern of thinking—a very familiar one. Somehow, if what I went through, even as a child, didn't seem as significant as what someone else was going through or had been through, I felt I didn't have a right to complain or talk about it or ask for help. As a child, I was even told that directly. "Think about the starving children in Biafra," my father would say at our dinner table when I didn't feel like finishing my food. "You have nothing to complain about. Think about so-and-so. Now that's someone who has it bad." Those messages of minimizing or diminishing my experience had been ingrained, and I was still doing it to myself.

I also looked at how, in our healing circle, I'd wanted to focus on health and healing rather than give any airtime to cancer. I'd wanted to avoid everything that included a focus on cancer, whether that meant acknowledging its existence or listening to those whose cancer had metastasized. Although we couldn't really do that in our group, I wished we didn't need to talk about cancer at all.

My need to focus on healing rather than cancer was steeped in the belief that what we focus on, we attract. Even more true was that I was scared shitless of cancer. I had a deep-seated fear that it would come back—a fear I tried to keep at bay and deny.

I also feared that I'd unknowingly "invite" it all in, both the cancer and its treatment, so that I could qualify as someone who had truly suffered. So that I would feel my experience was worthy.

171

Yet, as much as I didn't believe my experience had been as significant as others, I knew I didn't want to go through it again.

This thinking was crazy-making, but it was *real*. And whenever I let myself acknowledge what was there, it sent me into a spiral. So, to avoid that swirling, spinning dervish of thought that could take me to the depths of despair, I tried to avoid "all things cancer." With desperate intensity, I focused on healing.

It would take me a few more years to be able to sit with a woman undergoing treatment and be with her in her pain and suffering and fear. Thankfully, I would eventually get to the place where I could spend time with someone who was dealing with cancer and listen with compassion, where I could be present to and witness that experience. Eventually, I also came to be grateful for mine, but it was a grieving process that took time. There was no free pass through the grief—no way to jump forward and bypass the sadness and denial, the anger and bargaining. No way to skip over the fear of what could happen in the future. It had to be experienced—all of it—to be set free.

I'm Not a Survivor!

~

A bout two years after my mastectomy, I almost bit off the head of an unsuspecting woman. I was at a networking event, an evening gathering for female entrepreneurs held monthly in the founder's home. I was there to talk about the bath and body products I'd become involved with—clean products to pamper oneself, made locally and by hand. Products that wouldn't harm us or the planet.

As we vendors talked amongst ourselves, one woman who was there to promote her wellness business asked me, "So how long have you been in remission?"

My heart skipped a beat before beginning to pound in my ears. My breath caught in my throat. I hated the terminology we use to define ourselves related to cancer. Remission, survivor, fight, battle: These words describe a victim situation. To describe that we are powerless over the enemy—our enemy—cancer ... unless we fight and enter the battle of a lifetime.

Remission connotes an enemy lying in wait. Ready to attack at one's momentary weakness or when one has taken their eye off the threat. The enemy is patient and cunning, waiting until the precise moment one lets down their guard. Or retreats. Or goes to grab a cup of coffee or take out the garbage. Then, like a wild cat lying in wait, it pounces. And it usually attacks with a vengeance—far worse than the initial attack. This is the story we've bought into. And because we've come to believe it, that's exactly what usually happens.

Unless, of course, one makes it out five years. Then the medical community pronounces a person cured. Whether because it was completely eradicated or meds are being taken to keep the enemy behind enemy lines, at that five-year mark, one is deemed cured if the cancer has not reappeared.

So there I was, standing in the kitchen, the main character in a short film that had just been paused. I was at the two-year mark, not even halfway to when I'd be considered medically cured. Yet, I considered myself cured since my cancer had been completely removed and I'd needed no follow-up treatment.

I was caught off guard by this woman's question—the first time anyone had used the word remission in the same sentence as my past experience with breast cancer. In a matter of seconds that expanded to an eternity, I became angry and desperate to find the right comeback. I was not a survivor—I was a life thriver. And I was not in remission. Whether anyone else believed it or not, or would state it or not, I was cured. And that's exactly what I told her: "I am not in remission; I am cured." I paused and then added in a voice laced with venom for her audacity to ask such a loaded and presumptive question, "My cancer was completely removed."

"Oh, I'm sorry," she responded. "Well, I'm happy for you that your cancer is gone."

With that, I walked away, relieved to put distance between the two of us. Still fuming, I realized, though, that she'd just found my Achilles' heel. *Am I truly cured? Is the cancer really gone? Will it stay away?*

More than anything else, I wanted to be a life thriver, but I knew at that moment that I was still scared. I'd been covering up that fear with indignation. Yes, I would continue to refuse to buy into the language we use to talk about our relationship with cancer, but deep down, deep inside, I knew I was still afraid of the big bad wolf whose name started with "C." I was still trying to survive.

Bellisima Living

A year after I'd become a consultant for the local bath and body company, the business closed. The business model turned out not to be sustainable. Prior to closing, I'd already begun to create my own business, Bellisima Living, using an alternative spelling to the Italian word that inspired the name. *Bellissima* means "really beautiful" in Italian, and I wanted to help people create that kind of life. One that is *really beautiful* inside and out. I felt there was much more to address in addition to bath and body care products.

I began to create workshops so people could learn how to make their home environments safe using cost-effective, non-toxic products that are good for us and safe for the environment. I created a workshop to help people choose safer personal care products since our skin is our biggest organ, and everything we put on our skin is absorbed into our bloodstream. And I created workshops that helped people identify healthy food options. It was all about being informed, conscious consumers and learning how to plan and organize with intention.

Although I was eating a vegetarian diet at the time, I didn't tell people what to eat specifically but instead focused on what choices they could make that would be healthier for them and the planet. GMOs, for instance, were to be avoided as much as possible. I even created a shopping experience to introduce people to reading labels and identifying additives to avoid.

In six months, I'd created ten different workshops to encourage people to change where they spent their dollars and to help them support Mother Earth. In addition to workshops regarding personal care, household environment, and food, I included workshops to address recycling, repurposing, and implementation of energy-saving practices. My goal was to help people understand how our actions and choices can simultaneously help us and the planet. I felt good about all the information I'd researched and the ways I put that information together. I also felt good that I was aligned with the information I wanted to share—my family and I were living these practices daily. Of course, a big piece of what I created was intended to help people avoid cancer and other inflammatory illnesses.

Unfortunately, hardly anyone signed up. By the end of the first year, I'd had less than a handful of participants in workshops and taken two families on my shopping experience. Why weren't people signing up? I was networking to tell people about what I was doing, my workshops were affordable, and I was approachable. I worked hard not to come across as judgmental. People seemed genuinely interested and nodded in agreement during my thirty-second elevator pitches, but people weren't biting. What was wrong? Why weren't people interested?

During that year, independent of my business, I wrote a piece for a woman's anthology about my experience with breast cancer, and the following year, I offered to help a few of the women who were struggling with writing their stories for the second volume. The response I received after I'd helped each of them tell their stories was incredible. I'd been able to create a safe environment where they could share the difficult challenges they'd overcome without fear of ridicule or shame. They also felt that their stories had remained theirs—through our process, the women saw how their stories improved without losing their voices. Each woman was extremely grateful and proud to be part of a book of hope. I felt fulfilled as well, having supported them in revealing painful life moments and sharing how they moved beyond them.

Those experiences led to a huge internal awakening. I finally realized why Bellisima Living wasn't flourishing. My information was important, useful, and easy to access but had one underlying issue. It was fear-based. Everything I encouraged others to do, the ways I promoted changes in behavior, especially related to how and on what to spend their hard-earned dollars, was based in fear—to avoid the possibility of becoming sick from the products they used and the foods they consumed.

Change is difficult in any situation—under any circumstance. But change motivated by fear is even more challenging because it is not connected to a desire to improve or to feel lighter. Instead, it's about trying to avoid the heaviness of what can happen by not changing. Unless we are in a life-and-death situation (when fear motivates us to avoid true danger), most of us will run away, denying that a problem exists. Avoidance is a good solution to scary situations that are not immediately life threatening.

I also realized I was offering fear wrapped in anger. Admittedly, I was angry: at our world, at all that was happening to create a toxic environment and a toxic life, and all the ways we were disconnected from what was happening to our precious Mother Earth. I wanted people to wake up and change. I didn't think I behaved in a judgmental fashion, but I certainly judged the actions humans had taken and continued to take that harm us and our planet.

What was missing in my business was compassion. Compassion for people's fear of change, compassion for people's economic constraints, and most importantly, compassion for people's time constraints as they strove to balance work with taking care of their families. These were not excuses—they were *real* roadblocks to change.

What I was offering was just *too much*. People shied away because the information was heavy and potentially made them feel bad about what they could and could not do. Until and unless I could bring a genuine sense of understanding and patience to exactly where individuals were struggling, it would be difficult for people to open up to what I was "selling."

The experience of working with individuals to tell their stories of challenge and triumph opened me up to a whole new world of possibility. What I'd been able to bring to these women was the impact I couldn't seem to bring to my current business. I simply wasn't able to provide that compassion at the time. Deep inside, I was still angry and afraid of the *Big C*. Until that was healed within me, it would be almost impossible to bring heartfelt compassion, genuine love, patience, and acceptance to the idea of *bellissima living*.

Fear and Anger

As much as my external body had healed, my internal landscape was still in distress, filled with fear and anger. Fear of cancer returning, fear of chemotherapy and radiation—the two treatment modalities I'd been able to avoid—and fear of losing my life to cancer one day. And I was angry. Angry at what was being done to our food supply, angry at the environmental toxins we were exposed to every day—even when we did not use chemical products in our homes and yards, we were still exposed to toxic loads—and angry at the alternative healing modalities that continued to be available only outside the medical community. Still, mainstream medicine didn't accept nor integrate most alternative healing options. And the alternative community didn't necessarily want to play in the sandbox with mainstream medicine either. Yes, even though I denied it, I most definitely continued to live in fear and anger.

After working on stories for the second volume of the women's anthology and writing a second story of my own, I was asked by the two women heading up the project if I would start editing for them. They'd begun to help other authors self-publish, and they needed someone who could assist with the writing and editing of their stories. Would I like to join their team?

At first, I thought the idea was crazy. *Who am I to edit another writer's work? What training have I had to prepare me for this? I was not an English major, so what makes me think I can actually support an author through the writing-rewriting process and bring a level of expertise to ensure their book is the best it can be? What are they thinking ... that I could possibly do this?* The self-doubt kept flowing. I felt like an impostor to even consider offering my services as an editor.

Within a few days, though, other thoughts and feelings started to bubble up to the surface. Hadn't I written and edited in other capacities during my work-life career? Hadn't I written in the legal field, in the healthcare industry, and for a human resources department? Hadn't I written training materials and policies and procedures? I'd definitely done a lot of writing and editing within my past jobs. So why couldn't I do this? Besides, the women I'd worked with for the anthology had each expressed how comfortable and easy the rewriting process had been for them. So, wasn't I being given a message that this was a skill set, and maybe even an inherent gift, I could offer others?

I sat with the idea of editing for a few more days and then came to a decision. Yes, I'd be honored, thrilled, and simultaneously scared to death to begin working on authors' books. After having worked on the anthology stories that offered others hope and inspiration, I realized this was a way I could bring more healing to our world, to our planet. I truly had thought that helping people find ways to live greener, healthier lives was the work I was meant to do after having cancer, but it hadn't been right. This new opportunity showed me what that was: when I worked with someone on their writing, fear and anger were absent. I was able to work with my mind as well as my heart and intuition. And, most of all, my compassion rose to the surface to support each author as she told her story.

I knew every book would not be a memoir, but whether it was personal growth and development, fiction, a children's book, or some other genre, I had a sense that those same qualities and skills would be necessary. As much as I'd wanted Bellisima Living to succeed, I knew I had to let it go. A new door had opened, and it was time to step through into the light of living, loving, and serving others while tending to my own health and healing. I still had a long way to go.

I Bought a Boob Today ... Oh Boy!

Most women go shopping for lingerie every now and then, wanting to buy pieces of clothing to make themselves feel beautiful or sexy. Sometimes it's for more practical reasons—it's time to replace worn-out undergarments. For those of us who have undergone a mastectomy, there is a third reason. We need to buy new boobs as well as new bras to house them—sometimes even requiring new sizes of both. Post-mastectomy, I fit into this latter group.

I don't recall anything about the purchase of my first prosthesis post-surgery. I know I had to wear a supportive medical "corset" they gave me when I left the surgery center. I remember that once the chest tube had been removed, I stuffed one of my soft sports bras with some fabric and wore that instead. At some point in the healing process, I did get fitted for bras and a prosthesis, but that appointment and what I purchased seems to be part of the blur of those early months in my recovery. My second visit to the lingerie department, however, is still clear and vivid in my mind. Every time I think of that day, I hear the words, "I bought a boob today ... oh boy!" sung to the melody of the Beatles song "A Day in the Life."

Four and a half years post-op, I headed to the department store to meet with a fitter for our prescheduled appointment in the lingerie department. I wasn't looking forward to our meeting. In fact, I was dreading it. But after so much time, not only had my bras become ratty, but my silicone boob had lost its perkiness and become rather flat.

I knew it should have been replaced after two years, but I hadn't been ready to return to the store at that point, so I'd held off. Although the trained personnel make it a very "neutral" and supportive process, treating you as if there is nothing different about you, I'd shied away from going back. Somewhere inside, I wanted to deny that I needed a prosthesis and "special" bras. The crazy thing: I put on those bras and that boob every single day.

What got me to return to the store, more than my worn-out bras, was that I'd gained weight. My natural breast had become larger, enough so that I could see a difference between it and my fake boob. I'd become asymmetrical, and because I'm usually all about symmetry, I had to admit to myself that I needed a larger, fuller one.

Knowing that I wasn't looking forward to the experience, I asked my mom and sister to join my teenage daughters and me so we could all go to lunch afterward. At least we could have some fun in the process. And, not knowing exactly what to expect, I also needed the extra emotional support.

Once my fitter got me set up in my room, had me remove my top, and took my measurements, she went out to find just the right pieces to make me symmetrical once more. As I stood before the mirror, naked from the waist up and ready to try on the new bras she would bring back, I thought about my grandmother. In my mind's eye, I was standing beside her in my childhood bathroom and watched through the mirror as Nonna washed and got dressed. Thinking she might not notice that I was watching her every move, I tried not to look at her directly. After washing under her arms, she applied powder to her armpits. Bare-chested, she faced the bathroom mirror. The left side of Nonna's chest was dimpled. A purplish, jagged, crooked line revealed the path the knife had taken to cut away the malignancy. It was ugly. Yet, she continued to take care of her personal hygiene as if everything was perfectly normal.

How different I looked in comparison to Nonna. My scar was pencil-thin, straight, and white. It was almost completely faded into the rest of my skin. Shortly after the bandages had been removed, I'd shown it to my girlfriend, who was a nurse. She looked into my eyes with tenderness and strength I didn't yet possess. "Your surgeon did a beautiful job," she pronounced. Because of her words and with her standing next to me, I had been able to muster the courage to look at myself in the mirror for the first time back then. Now, I realized I had come to the place where I could look at myself with a sliver of acceptance. Admittedly, what stood before me was so much easier to accept than what Nonna had to come to terms with.

My fitter returned with the perfect bras and just the right prosthetic. She was amazing in her ability to get it right the first time. She helped me put on one of the bras and inserted the fake boob for me. I was symmetrical again! I put on the tight-fitting sweater I'd purposely worn for the occasion and went out to show the women in my family.

I felt a little strange as I pirouetted before them, yet excited as well. My chest was now sitting high, and my new boob closely matched the size of my real breast. It felt good to wear a bra that fit well and made me look perky once more.

"What do you think?" I asked almost shyly.

"You look good, Donna," my mother responded.

My sister added, "You look really nice."

"But do I look even?" I asked as I leaned over to make my back parallel to the ground, allowing them to see if my two mounds protruded equally. I stood back up.

"Well?" I prodded. "Do I look even?"

"Mom, you look good," one of my daughters responded impatiently. I knew they were more than ready to get to lunch.

My sister and mom chuckled. "Donna," my sister said, "yes, you look even."

Satisfied, I returned to my dressing room. Out of nowhere, I felt tears well up in my eyes. The smile I'd worn for my family came off. Momentarily, I felt the grief of my reality. Rather than showing off a sexy nightie, I had paraded myself fully dressed with some practical pieces of lingerie underneath—a fake boob and a bra that was somewhat pretty yet sensible— shaped so it could house my prosthetic. I dried my tears and tried to compose myself. I knew my fitter would be back at any moment.

As I took in some deep breaths, grace set in through the image of Nonna. Once more, we were back in my childhood bathroom, and she was continuing to get dressed for the day. Still facing the bathroom mirror, she put on her bra. Then, from the bathroom counter, she picked up the prosthetic of the 1960s—a tiny square pillow made of pastel-colored satin. She slipped it into the left cup of her bra. My eight-year-old self knew it was her "pretend" boob, the one she wore to look normal—and to hide her radical mastectomy.

I looked back at myself in the dressing room mirror. Rather than a square, slightly stuffed cushion, I was wearing a piece that looked and almost felt like a real breast. Instead of a patterned fabric, the exterior of my prosthetic was the color of skin.

Once the fitter returned and we finalized my purchases, I walked out feeling proud and grateful. As I approached my family, ready to move on to our lunch, I could sense Nonna at my side. She was smiling, and I could feel her love seeping in. In that instant, I knew. I would wear my boob with dignity, compassion, and even gratitude—for both of us.

Nonna

Nonna, did you cry when you lost your breast?
I cried.
Did it bother you to look at yourself in the mirror?
It bothered me.
Did you let your husband see you naked?
I stripped in front of mine.
Did he react with love and support?
Mine did.
Did you start to feel beautiful again?
I've begun.
Did you ever feel fear?
I've felt it often.
Did you ever worry you'd lose your other breast?
I have.
But things are changing …
Today, my fear is lessening.
Today, I have more acceptance for how I look.
Today, I have more compassion for what I've lived
through.
Today, I love myself.
Mostly.

Two Halves Make a Whole

N aked, I stand once more before my bathroom mirror. Nonna is again at my side. I finally see another piece of the puzzle. Family symmetry! She and I are the complement to one another. Nonna lost her left breast, and I lost my right. Suddenly I see the deeper meaning—maybe the true significance.

I am the bridge, the completion of a cycle of our family patterns. My intention is that my daughters will never have to experience what she and I, and even my mother, went through.

I am also the lucky one. The one who is able to find the tools and resources to go deeper. To look at the patterns in our family. To see what we, as women, coped with. To see our part in the dramas we each endured. To understand how we each held all of that pain—all our thoughts, feelings, and emotions, and every ounce of unworthiness—in our breasts. In the midst of all we tried to contain, we attempted to create harmony in our households. Even when the harmony was just an illusion, we worked to conjure more of it.

After coming to the United States from Italy, Nonna agreed to marry a man who was also from the Old Country. The two were introduced by Nonna's cousin, who ran a boarding house where Nonna and the man who became my grandfather were each living in San Francisco. The cousin encouraged Nonna to marry my grandfather after discovering that her own husband's eyes often wandered to my grandmother. After they married, Nonna soon learned she was living with a man who was angry about the way his life had gone. No one knew for certain what he'd left behind in Italy. My Nonno never spoke about his family or his life in the Old Country, and he seemed disappointed with his life in "the land of opportunity" as well. He never wanted to return to Italy, but he also wasn't content with his life in America. Nonno isolated in his San Francisco basement, where he made and drank his homemade wine, yet that behavior only amplified his resentment and hostility and created an environment where my grandmother and their two daughters walked on eggshells to make sure that "Papa" didn't rage.

My mother, Nonna's youngest daughter, married a man who had suffered terrible abuse as a child at the hand of a stepmother— both physical and mental—after losing his mother at the age of five. My father entered the army underage to escape his family life and served between WWII and the Korean War. He was involved in atom bomb testing in Eniwetok in the Pacific Islands and in the Nevada desert. Ultimately, he was stationed at the Presidio in San Francisco, across the country from where he'd been raised in Darby,

Pennsylvania. He never wanted to revisit where he'd grown up, yet those deep childhood wounds stayed with him and only seemed to be alleviated when he drank.

I, in turn, married a man who struggled with making a life in the United States after doors shut for him as a pilot in Greece. Feeling as if he had one foot in each country, he often felt like a fish out of water, not knowing who he was or where he fit in. He ultimately made a career as a commercial pilot in the US but unexpectedly lost his ability to fly almost twenty years before retirement age. Another life event that created a major setback, leading to extreme anger, grief, and depression. He didn't drink, but his pent-up emotions sometimes erupted in angry outbursts.

All three of us did our best to keep our families afloat—to smooth rough waters for our daughters as much as possible and to attempt to keep our husbands' ire at bay. And each of us paid a price for all we did as we tried to create an atmosphere of peace in our homes. Our breasts became the receptacles of our collective female pain as we endeavored to stave off and protect our children from the anguish suffered by our spouses.

I see Nonna looking on. She assures me that I am learning the lessons for all of us—for those who came before me and for those who will come after. I am opening my heart to what each of us lived through within the homes where we were raised and in the ones we created for ourselves and our families. With Nonna at my side, I am able to see our secrets, and I am willing to look at them. I am prepared to share our pain, our suffering, our shame, as well as our hopes and dreams—all of our truths—for the betterment of our family's future.

My hope is that my daughters and all who come after them will have a new path to follow. Sure, they will have challenges, obstacles, and even struggles—I am certain of that. It's happening already. But their difficulties can and most likely will be different. Maybe it will take less of their lifetimes to live through those trials and learn from them. And maybe, just maybe, they will be able to see their value, their inborn worthiness, and speak their truth sooner.

Nonna whispers in my ear. What she began, I am finishing. Her heart was filled with so much love and devotion to her family that she wasn't able to withstand all she had to endure to continue living. Nonna couldn't open the door, but with her at my side, I can. And I'm determined to put as much distance between me and cancer as possible.

Interlude

Broken

After having breast cancer in 2007, I believed I'd lost my voice years before my diagnosis. It seemed that I'd continued to move further away from who I was, from what I thought, from how I wanted to live my life, and from what I needed. To maintain a sense of calm and stability in our family, especially as we dealt with the loss of Dominic's aviation career in 2003, I tried to keep everything and everyone in control. I attempted to shoulder as much as I could of the emotional and economic burdens of our family without any regard for my mental and physical health. I lived and operated on autopilot survival mode.

In the process, the core of who I was went missing. I couldn't hear her anymore. She was lost, having retreated further within because life was too difficult for her to be present. The sensitive part of me couldn't risk being hurt, so she also receded further into the background, letting my mind run the show. My emotions were also lost and completely turned off. I seemed to stop experiencing feelings, and I avoided the unexpected by staying in the list of endless to-dos, responsibilities, and support of my husband and daughters.

Breast cancer was the wake-up call. Yet, thinking it was my voice that I needed to reclaim, I got louder and began to drown out the voices of others, including Dominic. I didn't want Dominic's opinions, and I didn't want to know how he felt. Most especially, I didn't want to hear his fears. I drowned him out and did my best to shut him out.

In 2008, we almost separated but decided to see if we could move past the challenges of the previous two years, including Dominic's realization that he could not continue with the job he'd taken two years earlier. Working in a cubicle, subjected to the almost daily corporate communiqués of how to be a company player, was not a place where he could thrive. He missed the cockpit and his ability to manage his own environment.

Even after he left the corporate job, the chasm between us continued to grow wider and deeper. We couldn't seem to find a way back to *us*. By 2011, we separated for a short time. As had happened two other times, once in the late eighties and once in the early nineties, we decided to try again. Yet, this time the divide between us was greater than ever before, and we seemed to remain strangers who only coexisted and interacted when it was about our teenage daughters. Even when it came to them, though, I tried to control things without his involvement. I strove to be the understanding parent I thought my girls needed—the kind of parent I thought I'd wanted. And I tried to avoid the possibility of his anger by not involving him. As much as possible, I kept him in the dark and powerless to act. In July 2012, we separated again, and this time we intended it to be "for good."

I blamed him for all our problems. For our daughters, who were angry and rebellious; for the anger and hostility in our home; for his lack of direction; for our lack of connection; for my lack of passion; for my hurt, my pain, and even for the cancer I'd had five years earlier. If he was out of my life, I believed everything would be good. The world would be right again. For a while, my way of seeing things seemed to be "right."

Shortly after we separated, Dominic asked to meet to go over the terms of our arrangement. He had a plan for moving forward, suggesting first that we not formally divorce so that I could keep his medical benefits. I was grateful for that offering and for him having thought of it—I hadn't gotten that far. Although I'd wanted us to part ways—and I was the one to say it out loud first, emphatically stating that I thought it was time to admit our marriage was over—I was still reeling from the immensity of this permanent solution. As much as I believed this was right for us and our daughters, the pain I felt was undeniable. Deep down, I had mixed feelings, but I was determined to move forward.

As we continued to review what he'd written out, we also could see the benefit of continuing to file our taxes together. Since neither of us intended to remarry, we agreed to live as a permanently separated couple. He proposed a monthly financial plan to meet our individual needs as well as a division of our property. It was all straightforward, logical, and more than fair. He did not want to fight, especially about money and property. Losing his family, on top of everything he'd lost with his career, was more than enough. He just wanted each of us to try to move on. I was too angry and hurt by all that had happened to see his generosity and care at the time. I was blind to his underlying message: for him, no amount of money could replace all he was losing—those he'd loved and been committed to—no matter what had gone on for him personally.

About ten months after we separated, he decided to go to Greece to live for a while. He wanted to see if he could make it his permanent home since his family and longtime friends all lived there. By summer, he was on the island of Paros with close friends of ours. During that time, our daughters turned eighteen and immediately moved out of our family home. For the first time in my adult life, I was living alone. I told myself this was what I needed—the opportunity to be on my own and learn to know and love me.

At first, the house became a calmer place. I could move about freely any time day or night, with no one else to consider: no more husband to navigate around, no more daughters to negotiate with, no more angry outbursts, no more threats of harm to themselves as they struggled with the pain of growing up. I could eat, sleep, and walk around naked when I wanted. I could go to the bathroom with the door open and play the piano whenever the impulse moved me, even in the middle of the night. I was free to do as I pleased. I told myself this is what I wanted—to create an independent life of peace and serenity and to begin to connect with the joy that had eluded me for so many years.

I began to do deeper inner work with my spiritual mentor, Janet, looking at patterns I'd allowed to grow and play a part in all that had happened to our family. The work wasn't easy, but it gave me hope for how my life might look in the future. Encouraged to enjoy life, I began to spend more time with friends. I continued to work. As months passed, I became more self-sufficient and self-reliant. It felt good, at least initially. Little by little, though, I had to admit that I was no closer to feeling joyful and at peace than I'd been when Dominic and I had been together. Having lost my marriage and feeling more estranged from my eighteen-year-old daughters, I carried intense grief and immense fear, and I was still deeply unhappy and dissatisfied with my life.

I'd been encouraged to go out with other men, even as friends, but I couldn't bring myself to do it. I continued to say I just wasn't ready and had no desire to create new relationships. I wanted to learn how to have a relationship with myself—to hear and know myself and to be able to enjoy spending time with only me. I wanted to learn to enjoy life, but it had to start with enjoying me. I had no idea when or if I would get there, but I had to try.

Marrying Me

I n March 2013, eight months after Dominic and I separated, on the occasion of our thirtieth wedding anniversary, I took myself to Pacific Grove, California. It was the place where we had been married and where we had taken our daughters many times to celebrate special occasions, including our anniversaries. I was determined to celebrate me and my life. I wanted to attach new memories and a new reason for coming to a place we'd loved as a family.

Before I left, a friend suggested that I might want to do what Jessie, the protagonist in *The Mermaid Chair,* had done: marry myself. I liked the idea. Maybe by marrying myself, I'd feel whole and happy and at peace with my life going forward. Maybe I'd find the joy that continued to elude me. Having read the book years earlier, I brought it along to remind me about what she had done.

Once I was settled into my motel room positioned at the edge of the eucalyptus-filled butterfly grove for which Pacific Grove is named, I let myself relax into my surroundings. I knew the best way for me to heal was to be nurtured by nature's gifts, and they were all around me. As sad as I felt about losing my marriage and our daughters losing their intact family, I told myself this was the best course of action. I was determined to move on—to say good-bye to what once was and hello to a new life, a new way of being and living. Most especially, to say hello to me.

The first evening, a doe grazed outside my window, unafraid of the people entering and exiting their rooms. She knew she was safe and could take time to enjoy the coolness of the evening and the lush vegetation that encompassed the grove. Her presence reminded me that I was here to nurture myself—to rest and nourish my body as I pondered a new direction.

The following morning, the day of our anniversary, I made my way to the office to grab some hot water. On the path was a dead monarch butterfly—one of the butterflies that had remained behind, having completed its life cycle. Even in death, her wings were brilliant shades of yellow, orange, and black, and she was majestic.

"Today is closure," I wrote in my journal. "I don't feel sad today. I feel hopeful. I see new horizons, new beginnings. The monarch showed me endings and beginnings. It is still beautiful and vibrantly colored in its death. It is still whole … I am too. I heard her message: 'Allow for the endings and new beginnings. Allow for your transformation. Invite it in. Be with it. Let what is next reveal itself to you—it is coming.'"

Later, I took a walk on the path through the grove, enjoying the wafting scent of eucalyptus and observing the fluttering butterflies whose final destination in their southward migration was this very spot. Whenever I've spent time in this grove, I've felt tremendous peace. This day was no different. I was home—not a final destination but a place of retreat.

As I made my way, a small eucalyptus branch on the ground ahead caught my attention. It was forked—two branches coming off of one. Was this a message that I had more than one path to choose from? I wasn't certain, but feeling compelled to keep the branch, I asked if I could take it with me. I got a message that it was here to support me. I also saw two blue jays and one raven as I made my way along the path, all squawking to get my attention. This was definitely a time to stay alert—change was coming, and I was not alone—synchronicity was everywhere.

On the evening of our anniversary, with pen and paper, I wrote a release of our marriage—releasing both of us to live lives filled with passion and purpose. It was my wish and my request that we both be blessed with happiness and serenity in our lives as we moved forward. It was also a declaration of release—that from my perspective, we were no longer bound to each other. We were free to find contentment, tranquility, and love, independent of each other. I offered hope that we would each find our way to joy-filled lives.

Then I took myself to a place at the water's edge where I could step into the tide pools and the rocks that led to where the ocean water flowed in and out. As I ripped the page into tiny pieces and threw them into the water, I asked Mother Ocean to take my words and release and bless us both. I watched until the last piece floated away, feeling a sense of peace and calm wash over me. It felt like the right action to take thirty years later at almost the exact time and within miles of where we had taken our marriage vows.

The following morning when I awoke, I decided this would be the day to make a commitment to myself. I took out my journal and began to write the words I would speak to myself—the vows I would offer to me. The words seemed to flow easily as I wrote about how I would care for myself physically, mentally, and spiritually; how I would show up in the world; and what support I would provide to myself so I could move forward with passion and purpose in my life. Once I wrote the words, I felt complete.

I realized I wanted an outward symbol of my commitment to myself—mainly to serve as a reminder of my vows to me. I'd seen a store in town that sold a wide array of jewelry, including rings, and I decided to go there to find a ring that I would place on my left ring finger. I wanted it to be different from my wedding ring—silver rather than gold and sans stones. Within minutes of arriving at the store, I found the perfect piece—a ring made of sterling silver with a unique, intricate, open design. I was ready for my ritual.

I arrived back at the beach, near the place where I had released our marriage the previous day. This time, I took a seat on a bench with a beautiful view of the water and the rocky shore below. With a sea lion who was sunning itself on a rock in the water as my witness, I read my vows out loud. I was ready to be good to myself, to practice self-care, to find ways to grow my passion, and to help myself heal further so that I could offer healing to others. I was ready to move forward and bring more joy into my life. At least, that is what I declared as the sun began to set.

When I got up to leave, I looked out at the water and my sea lion witness. She raised her flipper and waved. I smiled at one more synchronicity in a long line of magical moments. With a blessing and a goodbye, it was time to return home.

It's Harder to Find Me with You

A s time passed, more became apparent. My children were still angry and still rebellious—even more so with their father living in Greece. They demanded, and they defied. I soon saw how wishy-washy I'd always been, never taking a stance and holding to it. My caring and nurturing of them were without boundaries or limitations. They knew I could be easily persuaded to change my mind—I usually did. They knew I rarely, if ever, held my ground. Enough threats and negotiations from them, and I compromised or caved in completely. I wanted them to choose life and living, so anything I could do to make them not hurt themselves or not put themselves in harm's way, I did—even if it meant giving in. I believed I could control their choices by being easygoing and flexible.

I saw how their dad and I had both done this, giving in so they would at least be okay—happy would have been an even better outcome. I also began to see how much I had contributed to the state of our family—withholding from Dominic information that our daughters had confided in me. Yet, I often didn't have an opinion of my own and wasn't able to take a stance about what they were or weren't doing. As the secrets mounted, he was left in the dark—a significantly disempowering position. As a result, he became the bad guy, blowing up and venting after holding in his thoughts, observations, feelings, fears, and opinions for way too long. He was the one who tried to regain some semblance of control and order when I let things go too far.

It was also becoming apparent that I couldn't get happy, even on my own. No matter what I tried, joy eluded me. My guilt, shame, fear, and grief overwhelmed me to the point that I couldn't access anything else. I was deeply unhappy and dissatisfied with what I'd allowed to happen in my life and to our family.

The one place that was working in my life was my work; I'd become a successful editor. My editing work continued to expand, and eventually, I decided to start a publishing company to offer my clients a different publishing model. Being able to support and nurture others, helping them get out their messages and birth their books, became the place where I could put my energies and thrive. As an editor and publisher, my support was genuine and free from the dysfunctional methods I'd used to manipulate and control my home life.

In October 2013, about fifteen months after Dominic and I separated, he returned from Greece, and I offered him a place to stay while he decided whether to move out of state. Since both our daughters were no longer living at home, he took up residence in one of their bedrooms that had been turned into a guest room. Because we had never done anything to inflame our separation, we soon found a peaceful coexistence. I worked, and he cooked and helped around the house, even doing the grocery shopping and cleaning. We had polite and friendly conversations. Thinking he might move to Florida by January, we decided he would stay through the holidays. We intended to celebrate the holidays with our girls since we hadn't all been together the previous year.

When difficult events transpired with one of our daughters in early December, we soon found ourselves supporting each other. After she decided to cut off communication with the two of us and move out of state, we were able to grieve her loss from our lives together without any blame. We were both hurting and were able to share our grief. We didn't know what the future would bring, but we hoped we could find a way to reconnect with her.

During that time, a shift began for both of us, but most dramatically for me. I had been the one who asked him to leave in July 2012, and now I was the one who posed a different question in early January 2014, one I never imagined I'd hear myself speak: "Do you think it's possible for us to find our way back to each other? I don't know, but with all that has happened over the past few months, I feel closer to you than I have in years. Doesn't it also mean something that in the past eighteen months, neither of us attempted to date anyone else, and we haven't done anything to make this separation permanent? Do you think it's possible for us to get back together? I never thought I'd say this, but I'd like to try. I'd like to at least explore what that might look like."

It was one of the first times in a long while when I knew what I wanted, at least what I wanted to explore. And I'd said it out loud—without any game playing, any passive-aggressiveness, any manipulation, or any need for self-protection. I was straight and direct. I let my heart show through—my sensitivity and vulnerability exposed.

"That is what I've hoped for all along … and why I agreed to stay here. I truly hoped we could find our way back together. I never wanted to stay apart," he admitted.

What revelations! Who would have thought that this is where we'd be? I sure hadn't.

I ended by saying, "You know what? I believe continuing to figure out who I am and what I want will be much more difficult to do in relationship with you, but I want to do it if you are willing. Being myself and finding the real me may seem easier to do alone, but I don't think it will be as authentic. The real challenge is finding the *real me* when I'm with you. I honestly think that is what I'm meant to do."

With those words spoken out loud, I knew it was true. My challenge had been to find me, to be me, and to allow me to show through while I am "with you." To be clear about who I am and allow that to come through rather than to never know what I actually think and feel when I'm in the midst of listening to another's voice, another's feelings, another's desires, and most especially, when dealing with a crisis. This has been part of my lifelong learning. And apparently, I wasn't yet done with the lesson.

Respite and Reprieve

Since the previous September, I had been experiencing rectal pain and bleeding. I thought it was nothing—an internal cut or maybe hemorrhoids. I'd had both issues in the past. By November, the issue had worsened.

Since the previous May, while Dominic had been in Greece, life had been challenging. During those months, I'd hired people to get the house ready to sell, and I'd also done some of the work, like painting bedrooms and bathrooms neutral colors, with the help of friends. Focusing on a long to-do list left little time for me to think about my life and my future—other than the potential to downsize and live in a home with no "Mazzitelli family" history. I planned to have the house on the market by July.

Our daughters were angry about the disruption to their lives with Dominic's and my separation and the potential that their family home would be sold, and they wanted to get as far away from it all as possible. On the day of their eighteenth birthday, one left for Boulder that morning and wouldn't return for even a visit during the following six months. The other daughter spent her birthday with her boyfriend and came over briefly in the evening for birthday cake. By nightfall, I was alone in my bedroom, crying for all that was lost—an intact family, a relationship with our daughters, and a marriage that had recently hit the thirty-year mark during our separation. Although I claimed to have a new direction, I was floundering, hanging on by a thread to the potential of a new life.

As Dominic and I talked about all that had transpired during that time, including the challenges I'd dealt with related to each of our daughters and my attempt to sell our family home, he suggested I take a trip. He knew I needed time to tend to myself physically, emotionally, and spiritually. For once, I listened to him and admitted he was right.

Since he was now staying in our home, he could watch our animals. I decided the warmth and nurturance of Kauai, our favorite Hawaiian island, would be perfect. I quickly made plans to take off in early November. I had work that needed to be completed by Thanksgiving, but I'd still have plenty of downtime to take in the ocean, sit on the beach, and spend time in Hanalei Bay, my favorite little beach town. Secretly, I hoped that the rest and time away would heal whatever was going on with my body, but if I was still dealing with issues, I promised myself I'd address them when I returned.

Soon enough, I was on my way with my computer, bathing suit, sunglasses, and a beach towel. My rented one-bedroom condo overlooking the Pacific Ocean awaited me. Once I arrived, though, things got worse with my physical health. I couldn't leave the bathroom for long, so I stayed in my condo more than I'd planned. My symptoms became more pronounced, and I could no longer deny that something was terribly wrong. I researched what could possibly be happening and came up with a range of diseases and conditions, from hemorrhoids to IBS.

Closing the Chapter to Begin a New One

For almost a year, between 2012 and 2013, I'd contemplated how to commemorate the ending to the chapter of my life that had begun in 2007 with my cancer diagnosis. I decided the best way to close that chapter and symbolically signify the beginning of a new one was a tattoo. It would be placed where my right breast had once been.

At first, the main reason for considering a tattoo had been to hide the scar. I had to admit, though, that my scar was almost beautiful, so pencil-thin and faint that it was barely noticeable. A testimony to the craftsmanship of my female surgeon. If I had one complaint, it was the length. My scar stretched from just above my sternum to below the start of my armpit. It was longer than I'd ever expected.

My other reasons had been related to vanity and shame. I'd envisioned what it would be like to get naked and offer my body to another man, should Dominic and I decide to make our separation permanent. Wouldn't I and my body be more appealing if I had a tattoo rather than a missing breast?

"Get over it!" Janet said to me one day when, during our separation, I wondered if any man besides Dominic would ever find me attractive. "I've seen three-breasted women dancing naked as if it were the most normal and natural thing in the world. Get over yourself!"

She also told me that a tattoo is a sacred piece added to our bodies. "It's important that what you put on your body has deep significance to you." Not only the "what" of a tattoo, but the "when" of it would be important. I realized the "who" would be critical too. Not just because of hygiene, but it would have to be someone who did beautiful body art and understood the profound meaning of this tattoo for me.

I let many months pass. I still didn't know what images I wanted or who would ink my tattoo. I still wasn't clear about why I even needed to do it. It seemed that maybe the why would be related to the image I chose. Since I didn't yet have clarity about any of it, I stopped dwelling on my potential tattoo. But the idea of getting one never left me.

Then came my impromptu trip to Kauai. One morning as I ordered my mocha from the local coffee house in Hanalei, I noticed that two of the women had the most beautiful tattoos I'd ever seen. "Billie across the way did them. She's awesome!" one of the women told me. *Hmm*, I thought, *I think I need to visit Billie.*

The urging wouldn't stop, and soon enough, I found myself climbing the stairs to the second-story office of Blue Tiki Tattoo.

I walked in and immediately saw her—a woman whose entire body tells stories. I approached the counter, not sure what I was doing and with no plan of what I was going to say. I blurted out, "Uh, I met Sara across the street, and she said you did her tattoos. They're beautiful! I've been thinking about getting a tattoo for almost a year … where my mastectomy was done. I think you might be the person who is supposed to do it. I know I want a panther and a monarch butterfly … and some kind of flower …" I rambled on.

Billie listened, asked questions to be sure my mastectomy hadn't been done recently, and told me she was about to take off for three days after having worked twelve straight days in a row. My excitement crashed. "I'll be back on Saturday," she added. "We could do it then. I don't have anything scheduled so far."

"I leave on Sunday. Would that work to travel the day after I get a tattoo?"

She explained that I'd have enough time to care for it before I left. She said she would instruct me about how to tend to it on the day I traveled home and beyond. After looking through books of designs, I didn't find what I wanted, so she suggested that she draw some designs during her time off. She'd have at least two versions to show me on Saturday. We looked back at some of the images so she could get at least some idea of what I had in mind. She also asked to see my chest and was impressed at how faint my scar was. I scheduled my appointment for eleven in the morning on Saturday. I decided I wouldn't tell anyone what I was planning to do. This was my experience, my decision, and I didn't want anyone to influence either. I was nervous and excited, about to go through an experience that was so far from anything I'd done in my life, so I needed to just be with myself through the process.

Two days later, I went to see a woman who worked in the office next to the tattoo shop for some energetic body work. Since I was still suffering from bowel issues, I thought bodywork might help clear the problem. In that session, I saw more of the pain from past experiences that I needed to release and shift. Most especially, that pain related to how I saw myself and the life I'd lived so far. Toward the end of the session, she guided me through a meditation. In it, I saw a lotus flower. "You are beautiful," it told me. "Just like me, you are beautiful because you are, because you exist. You have to do nothing but BE."

I came out of that meditation deeply moved, and I knew what flower had to be included in my tattoo—a pink lotus. I had thought the kind of flower I would include might represent my maternal grandmother or my mother, who had both had cancer. Or the flower might represent my twin daughters, who I hoped would never have to experience breast cancer since I believed I was the one to break the patterns tied to this disease. After the meditation, however, I knew the flower had to be for and about me—only me. I realized the lotus flower was the symbol of how I needed to see myself—coming from the murk and gunk, still growing from that place, yet complete and beautiful in its bloom. Pure *I AM* manifestation. I saw cancer as a part of my past, a part of the murkiness I was emerging from. Although still in physical discomfort because of my current bowel issues, I was ready to transform my past into a beautiful present.

Later that day, I sat on the beach at Hanalei Bay and journaled about my experience with the bodywork. Three young women passed in front of me—the middle one I thought I recognized. She turned out to be Bethany Hamilton, the young woman who lost her left arm when a shark bit it off while she and her friends were out surfing in the early morning. I'd seen *Soul Surfer* with my daughters and had read more about her after the movie. I knew she was now married and continued to live in Hanalei.

I wanted to approach her to get her autograph for my girls but stopped myself. She was out for a walk and bodysurfing with her girlfriends. I didn't want to disturb that. Then it struck me—the reason I saw her. It was not for my daughters or an autograph. Once again, it was for me—a continuation of the message that began during my bodywork session. "You are beautiful. With or without an arm, with or without a breast, we are all beautiful."

In that moment, I knew it *was* time to get my tattoo. I knew why I was doing it, what it would be, and what it represented. I had gotten the final piece of information. This tattoo was for me. Yes, I had ultimately decided to have a mastectomy, and yes, I had come to accept how my body looked. I no longer saw my missing breast or my scar as grotesque. I had long ago made peace with my experience. Now, however, I had the chance to transform that experience and what I'd been left with, into beauty—a meaningful, personal work of art I could appreciate and admire each day when I looked at myself in the mirror. I could create *symbology* for who I'd become as a result of my mastectomy and all that had happened since then. And most of all, I could take what had been one of my most difficult life moments and transform it into something beautiful for me to have always. When I returned to my condo, I emailed Billie with a sample image of a pink lotus flower, letting her know this was the flower to incorporate.

I arrived at the shop on Saturday morning, nervous and apprehensive, but as soon as I saw the drawings she'd created, I was certain about what I was doing. Billie was the one, and this was the day. It was time to close one chapter to begin a new one.

Five hours later, Billie and I were bonded for life. She had felt the tremendous sacredness of what we were doing together, and I had been transformed inside and out as she inked the imagery onto my chest, sometimes singing to carry me along as she worked. I was lulled by her voice and her strong yet gentle presence. At other times, she was silent, knowing I needed to go inward and be immersed in the experience.

Just as my body began to shake, an involuntary reaction to the number of hours needed to create this body art, Billie smiled down at me. "It's done," she told me. "Take your time to sit up, and when you're ready, we'll walk over to the mirror so you can see how it turned out. It's beautiful, and so are you," she added.

After I sat up and drank some water, I stood for the first time in many hours. Looking down at it while she'd worked, I could tell how beautiful it was, but now I was ready to see the complete artwork, which wrapped to my armpit. Billie guided me over to a mirror on the wall. I couldn't believe how beautiful and amazing it was. The colors were vibrant, and the imagery was even more incredible than what she'd drawn on paper. Pink lotus floated in rippling water, reminding me of unconditional love and the meaning of the lotus—a beautiful flower that grows up out of the silt, murk, and gunk; a living, breathing reminder that beauty can grow from pain. Panther, her blue-black face with amber eyes that mirror my own, emerged from behind the lotus flower, reflecting the inner power, courage, and strength that reside within me and reminding me of the need for structure and boundaries within my life. Monarch, a symbol of transformation, hovered just out of panther's reach at panther's eye level—the butterfly's profile representing what had been transformed and inviting me to continue to evolve.

Tears of gratitude streamed down my cheeks as we both admired her work and took in the significance of our time together. With tears in her eyes, Billie told me she'd called her mother that morning to tell her about me. She confessed that she'd started to cry to her mom, feeling the awesome responsibility to do this art for me and to see it through to completion. She'd been humbled by my willingness to do such an elaborate design, not having any previous experience with inking. She wanted to find a way to ensure that I could handle it and confided in her mom that she was scared I'd get up from the table and walk out before we were done.

We learned a lot from each other that day, as well as even more about ourselves. I found out that I had an inner strength and the ability to persevere that went beyond emotional struggles. I could tolerate intense physical pain. And Billie ... well, she found out how powerful her intuition and inner knowing were. As an artist working on a human body rather than a canvas, she sensed when I needed to be sung to—a lullaby of sorts to wash over me and distract me from the discomfort—and when I needed absolute quiet to go inward to stay focused and ride the waves of intense pain.

Someday I plan to return to Kauai and to Billie so she can add to my tattoo. I believe I already know what needs to be inked on top of the scars left by the drains that were placed in my chest—a beautiful red hibiscus flower that will sit underneath the monarch butterfly. But who knows? Maybe by the time I get back, a new image will reveal itself.

That's the beauty of life. At every turn of a new day and within the moments of each day, more is revealed. What was may no longer be. And what has always been may become even clearer. With an open mind and heart and with eyes eager to see, a gift more beautiful than we could have imagined may present itself. And that source of beauty may turn out to be a deeper understanding of who we are. With those thoughts, I was ready to get back to Colorado and move forward with my life. I was excited for the future.

Hemorrhoids

When I left Hawaii with the symbol of my internal transformation, I was certain that what was going on physically would be easily addressed and resolved, especially after my brief time away and even my time with the energy healer. I came home ready to deal with it—whatever *it* turned out to be.

On the Wednesday before Thanksgiving, I went to see my primary care physician. After doing a digital examination, the nurse practitioner said she didn't feel any hemorrhoids or anything that seemed out of the ordinary. Because of the bleeding I was experiencing, she thought it was a GI bleed, but that didn't fit for me. Based on what I'd read, it didn't match my symptoms. Since we were about to start the long Thanksgiving weekend, she advised that I go to the ER to have a workup. I decided to wait until Friday, the day after the holiday. The ER diagnosed it as hemorrhoids and gave me a referral to a surgeon. I was relieved. Even though I was in pain and still experiencing spasms and bleeding, I knew my life was not in jeopardy. I decided to wait and address it after Christmas, anticipating that I would need to have surgery to remove them. My mother had undergone a hemorrhoidectomy decades earlier, so I was certain I'd go through a similar procedure.

Unfortunately, with all that had transpired over the holidays related to one of our daughters, January turned into February, and I was finally ready to face a medical procedure. I made an appointment for Friday, February 7.

Within a day of scheduling the appointment, Dominic received a phone call. Willy, the husband of a close friend of ours, wanted to invite us to the surprise birthday weekend he was planning. He wanted to make us the surprise guests of honor since we all hadn't seen each other in years. He knew Tony would be blown away by our arrival. Our presence would also serve another purpose: a diversion from the big birthday bash he was planning.

Tony had been the best man at our wedding thirty-one years earlier; he and Dominic had become friends years before that, having gone through flight training at the same flight school in California and working as flight instructors together. Ultimately, they flew for the same airline.

Dominic and I talked about how wonderful it would be to celebrate Tony's birthday with him after all these years. Tony had always been a big supporter of both of us and our marriage. So, although we weren't yet officially back together, we decided to go. I called and rescheduled my doctor's appointment for the following Friday.

We'd been discussing for weeks our impending recommitment and what our new relationship would look like but had not yet written our commitment letter—a detail we'd decided would be important for us to have. Taking time away in Florida to celebrate the birthday of our best man would bring us back to the beginnings of our marriage commitment and allow us to hit pause as we continued to redefine our relationship moving forward. Most of all, it would provide a much-needed break from all we'd gone through over the holidays.

Off we flew to spend time in the warm Florida climate, hanging out on the beaches in Fort Lauderdale, eating great food, and participating in the surprise celebration that started with our arrival. Of course, my condition came too, but since I knew it would be dealt with soon enough, I was able to set aside my concerns and enjoy our mini-vacation and the rebuilding of us.

Commitment

Through January and into February, Dominic and I had talked about our relationship. We went through a process of identifying what we each need—in any relationship with anyone. Many of the items that showed up for us individually were related to what had gone wrong in our relationship. We both listed honesty, which meant never withholding information; taking time to connect emotionally and physically; placing our relationship above other relationships, including with our daughters; making plans, including travel; and having a home where peace and calm reign. Financially, we had done all right, but we both wanted more financial freedom to support our desire for entertainment and travel.

What was especially interesting was how our lists, which we'd created independent of each other, were almost identical. When we got together to share what we'd identified, we found that most of what we require in a partnership was the same. The priority looked different on a few items, but our lists were alike. Through this exercise, we saw how we were more similar than different from each other. We also saw how much we'd each grown in our time apart and how willing we'd become to look at our own stuff.

It was finally clear that we'd both contributed to the demise of our marriage. It was not one person's fault. Of course, it never really is. We also acknowledged that our time apart had been necessary. We would never have made our way back to each other had we not separated for as long as we did. And not having done more to hurt each other further—or to retaliate for the ways we each thought we'd been wronged and for the pain we each felt we'd endured—had been crucial to finding ourselves and where we were now.

From our independent lists, we created a commitment letter indicating what we would do and what we intended our marriage to look like from that point forward. We chose not to further re-hash the past and not to put our rings back on. Our commitment letter would bind us together and propel us forward into the future. Our commitment to each other would be what we wore outwardly. Should we ever decide we wanted another outward symbol, we'd decide together what that would be.

We signed our letter on February 13, 2014, one day before Valentine's Day. We were both ready to move forward with an *updated* vision for our relationship that included foundational elements we now saw in a *new* way: Commitment. Recommitment. Connection. Dedication. Being bound together … from this day forward. Until death do us part.

Second
Movement

Panther's amber eyes looked into mine.

"I am here with you.

It is no accident you created me at this moment in time.

I am here to remind you of

your internal power—your internal knowing.

You have everything you need to traverse

this part of your life's journey," she said.

"It is only a part of your life's story—and only for a brief time.

But there is much to learn.

You must be swift and focused.

And remember, you are not alone."

Valentine's Day ...
Take 2

R efreshed from our time away and feeling closer to Dominic than I had in many years, life felt good ... really good. He and I had signed our commitment letter and created a symbol in our home for our new relationship. We were filled with happiness, hopefulness, and a sense of peace for where we'd come and where we were going.

I'd never imagined being together again, yet here we were, looking at each other with an intention of vulnerability and full disclosure as well as open hearts. We'd both come home to each other and to our house in Castle Rock, and it felt wonderful. We'd learned a lot in the past, together and apart, and now we were ready to continue this life journey with each other.

We looked forward to our thirty-first anniversary in March and decided to fly to Paris and London—places we'd never visited together. I'd never been to either European city and always dreamed of visiting both. Dominic had been to Paris when he was a child, but he'd been so young that he didn't have any memories of his time there. After spending the previous thirtieth anniversary apart, and the anniversary prior to that filled with tension and discord, we were both ready to truly celebrate our marriage and our recommitment to each other. But first, I needed to address my physical health.

I told Dominic I'd go to my appointment alone since I expected it to be pretty straightforward. If it wasn't hemorrhoids, it most likely was a fissure—I'd read about them, and my symptoms seemed to fit. No longer trying to control his involvement, my decision had more to do with truly believing this would be an easy issue to address. He made plans to have lunch with our daughter who was living in Denver, and we agreed to meet back at our house by mid-afternoon.

I walked into the surgeon's office and was greeted by a kind receptionist who handed me paperwork to complete. Within minutes of handing back the forms, the surgeon's assistant came out to get me. She took me into a spacious exam room bordered by dark brown wooden cabinetry and matching furniture. Except for the narrow exam table on the back wall, it could have been a generic office or meeting room. Nothing about it felt medical—and especially not surgical. After initial questions to confirm the reason for my visit, she told me the doctor would be in shortly. She explained that I didn't need to change yet, as he would start with a consult.

As I waited for the doctor, I noted how different my behavior was compared to how I'd behaved with the medical assistant seven years earlier. The surgeon's assistant and I had exchanged pleasantries, and I felt gratitude that I was there to resolve my condition. I was relieved to finally address what I believed was simply an inconvenient problem. I was ready to stop seeing blood in the toilet bowl and to stop feeling discomfort when I was seated.

The surgeon came in shortly after the assistant left and extended his hand. "Hi, I'm Glenn. It's nice to meet you, Mrs. Mazzitelli."

"Please call me Donna," I responded, feeling relaxed in his presence. I could sense his warmth and sensitivity, rare qualities in surgeons, based on my past experiences.

Once more, I described my symptoms. He said, "I'm sure from your description that we are dealing with a fissure rather than hemorrhoids. Your symptoms fit that perfectly. Why don't we go ahead and do an exam to confirm?"

He handed me a gown and asked me to change. He said he'd answer any and all of my questions once he confirmed what he suspected. Glenn left the room, and as I changed, I let out a huge sigh of relief. I couldn't deny that I'd been worried about having waited too long. Glenn's pre-exam suspicions indicated I was going to be fine. This would be easy to deal with. Allowing myself to relax, I lay on my back on the table as he'd instructed and awaited his return.

When he reentered the room, he smiled and came over to where I lay. He put on gloves, turned on his exam light, and moved it as he asked me to turn onto my side facing the wall. He then placed his index finger inside to feel around. "Hmm," he said.

"What is it?" I asked, sensing the change in his tone.

"Well, it is definitely not a fissure," he told me. He paused as he continued to examine me, adjusting the light for a better view.

"No, this is not a fissure. You've got a tumor in here," he added as he continued to explore the area. He withdrew his hand, and with a very distressed look on his face, continued. "I hate to have to tell you this, but this is cancer."

My breath caught in my throat as I closed my eyes. A tear escaped and rolled down my cheek to the table I was lying on. *This can't be happening! It just can't be!* I tried to compose myself before opening my eyes. Looking at the blank wall in front of me, I let his words swirl around and finally settle in my body, landing at my gut. I felt like throwing up. Just as when I was a child and tried to blend into the wall to avoid getting a shot, I once more wished I had that ability. *You've got to be kidding! He's got to be wrong! As nice as he seems to be, he* has *to be wrong!*

I turned myself onto my back so I could look directly at him, and with as much calm and courage as I could gather, I inhaled deeply before speaking. "Are you sure? Couldn't it be a benign growth?"

"I've seen a lot of tumors, and this is, unfortunately, cancer. It is a solid mass, hard, and there is a lot of blood ... there's a large blood supply to it. I know this is not what you were expecting to hear. It wasn't what I expected to find either," Glenn said, obviously distraught. It was apparent in the saddened look on his face and the sound of his voice, which had gone from upbeat and cheery to gravely serious. "Why don't you get dressed, and we can talk some more?"

Shocked and in complete disbelief, I got up and dressed mechanically, feeling and thinking about nothing other than, *He's got to be wrong. This just can't be. There is no way this is happening!*

Glenn came back, and we sat facing each other. "I know this is not what you expected to hear," he repeated. He asked me to explain what they'd told me at the ER in November. I ended by asking, "Have I put myself in jeopardy because I didn't come in sooner? I really thought it was hemorrhoids, as they said, or a fissure, based on my research."

His face flushed. Although he spoke almost methodically, his anger was palpable. "You believed what you were told. I can understand and appreciate deciding to wait based on what they said. And I don't think you've put yourself at risk. We'll get you scheduled for a colonoscopy and do a biopsy at the same time. We'll make sure there is nothing else going on besides the one tumor."

"Is there any possibility it isn't cancer?" I wanted so badly to believe he could be wrong. I just wanted the chance for it to be anything but cancer.

"I know how hard this is, and I wish I could tell you that it isn't cancer, but no, I do not believe there is any possibility. As I said, because of its characteristics, I am certain this is a cancerous tumor. I've seen a lot of them in my years of practice. The biopsy will confirm what I suspect. It will also give us a little more info. From the exam, I believe it is about four centimeters in size. The colonoscopy will give us accurate measures as well. I am so very sorry."

"Thank you," I replied, seeing how distressed he was over the outcome of his findings. What I especially admired about him was his compassionate directness. He spoke the truth, but he did it with care. I could see how visibly upset he was. Because of what I'd told him about my previous diagnoses, he had not expected to find a tumor. That was obvious from his facial expressions, tone, and demeanor. They'd both been wrong: the nurse practitioner who said she felt nothing and then days later an ER doctor who told me he was certain I had hemorrhoids.

Cancer! The word I never expected to hear again, especially related to *my* body. Yet, here I was, facing a new diagnosis.

Trying to grasp the situation, I walked out after scheduling my colonoscopy. I appreciated his assistant's kind words, "I'm so very sorry," that she said when I told her I'd never imagined hearing that diagnosis again … and, maybe even worst of all, for the second time on Valentine's Day.

I made my way to my car, knowing what I had to do next: call Dominic. I sat in the driver's seat, staring ahead. I could not believe what I needed to say to him. Especially just after recommitting to each other the previous day. How could I now tell him I have cancer? How could I burst the bubble of all we were looking forward to? Intimacy—physical and emotional—trips, travel, my increased work life and his committed support of the work I was doing, our daily life as empty nesters. All of the words in our written commitment were related to how we wanted to create and live our life together. Nowhere on the page was anything about cancer or illness. We'd focused on health and our desire to support our mental and physical well-being. My body apparently had other ideas.

The tears flowed as I wondered how this had come to be. I'd learned the lessons, hadn't I, from my first experience with cancer? But if I hadn't, what else did I need to learn? Why was cancer my teacher once more? I sat there, trying to regain my composure. I knew I wouldn't be able to form words if I called immediately, not decipherable ones anyway. And how would I start the conversation? "Hi, you'll never believe it, but I've got cancer *again!*" Was there any way to ease into this news? Not really. But first, I knew I had to get calm.

I remembered my phone conversations the first time when it seemed I might have breast cancer. First to Dominic, second to my best friend in California, Denise. This time, I would only make one call to Dominic. The last time, they hadn't used the word "cancer" initially, but I believed it was cancer because of what they weren't saying. This time, the doctor had been straight with me as he provided enough information for me to grasp the reality of my situation. No questions to ponder, no false promises to grab onto. This time it was clear—I have cancer, and what will come next is determining whether it's anal or rectal cancer, or more extensive than that: colon cancer. I didn't know what that meant, but he'd indicated that each has a slightly different course of action. He ended by saying, "Let's wait and get the results before we talk about what comes next." Even he apparently had his limits for how far he'd go with his pronouncements. It was obvious he wanted to discuss facts rather than suppositions. I'd clearly had enough of that already.

I grabbed my phone from my purse and slid my finger across the screen. It was time to make the call. Dominic was still with our daughter Alex when he answered. "Hi," I said in response to his greeting. "Well, I saw the doctor, and it's not what I expected or what you signed up for. He said it's cancer. It's a tumor, and he's sure it's malignant."

Silence. The tears came to my eyes as I took a breath.

"Whatever it is, we'll deal with it. I'm here, and we'll get through this together. Whatever it turns out to be, we'll face it together. Okay?"

"Okay," I whispered back.

I knew I meant it this time. No more warrior woman. No more defiance. No more my way or the highway. This time, I would let him in and allow him to be a part of whatever lay ahead. This time, I would let him help me. I needed that. He needed that. We might not have written down, "in sickness and in health," but we'd said that over thirty years earlier to each other. And now we'd committed to being together once again, sharing in whatever would unfold in our lives, being truthful and honest and open with each other—a commitment to full disclosure without any secrets. The framework was there to face whatever happened in our life together. I just hadn't expected "it" to be so soon or to be cancer. The Universe obviously had other plans.

We ended our call, and I drove toward home as tears spilled from my eyes. This was an opportunity for a do-over on so many levels—cancer, treatment decisions, integration of treatment modalities, openness to the journey ahead, acceptance, and most especially, allowing others in. This time I would ask for and let others help. This time I had to admit I needed it—spiritually, emotionally, and physically. This time I couldn't and wouldn't go it alone. On this Valentine's Day, I vowed to keep my heart open. It was the greatest gift of love I could give myself.

Colonoscopy Day

Exactly one week later, Dominic and I stood at the desk of the surgery center to check in. I graciously took the forms they gave me to complete and found a chair. I use the word "graciously" because so often in the past, I'd taken forms with a look of indignation and impatience. Today I was once again ready to let down my guard and allow the staff to help me.

When they asked for a copay as I turned in my paperwork, I was ready to make a comment like, "Really, you want our money at a time like this!" but I didn't. This was a business, after all. Even though I wondered what was in store for my life, I knew they needed to manage the business side of things, which meant collecting money. I took a seat and let Dominic handle it, letting go of the need to be righteous or in control.

We waited together for about ten minutes, and then a woman appeared out of a side door and called my name. It was time. I kissed Dominic, my newly regained life partner, and asked him to hold the sacred bundle I'd brought along to support me—a piece of cloth wrapped and tied around objects from nature. Not sharing my spiritual path, he took the bundle as if it were the most natural thing to do and placed it in his pocket. Without question or judgment, he would be my support in every aspect of what lay ahead.

I'd been through two colonoscopies previously, so I knew the drill. As I got on the gurney in my hospital gown and we discussed the arm that had to be used for my IV because of my mastectomy, one of the nurses noticed the edge of my tattoo. I told her what it symbolized and how I'd come to acquire it. I lowered my gown and showed it to the two nurses who were there to do my prep. "Beautiful!" they both exclaimed.

As we continued to talk, I realized I'd already brought some much-needed light to a place where not much conversation or illumination goes on. A friend of mine who had been an endoscopic nurse told me years earlier how working endoscopy had dulled her spirit. Being with sedated patients in a small room with staff and a doctor who didn't speak about anything but what was necessary to film the patient lying on their side had numbed her to life and living, joy and passion. She ultimately retired early and changed careers. I thought of her as these women thanked me for sharing a part of myself with them.

Soon enough, I was sedated, and the procedure was underway, none of which I remember. Once I was able to walk and they were certain I'd come through the colonoscopy with flying colors, they took me to Dominic. He told me that while I was in recovery, my surgeon had come and spoken to him. Everything looked good inside except the one tumor. The biopsy was being sent to the lab. The surgeon was certain it was malignant. What he was less certain about was whether this was anal or rectal cancer. Because of the position of the tumor, it could be either, he explained to Dominic. The biopsy would give them the answer. Anal and rectal cells are different, he said. "Let's hope this is anal cancer. That is much easier to treat and gives us a good prognosis."

Dominic recounted all of this to me before we headed home. At that point, neither of us really understood the difference in diagnosis, treatment, or prognosis. We only knew that we'd just begun this journey, and we definitely had a long road ahead.

Within a few days, we sat in front of the surgeon at his alternate office. I'd now met this man in three different locations. The diagnosis was anal cancer, undifferentiated squamous cells. He explained: "Undifferentiated is not exactly a good thing; however, I am happy that we aren't dealing with something aggressive or a tumor that progressed into your rectum."

This was pure "unadulterated" anal cancer. I didn't understand what undifferentiated cells meant, but I did understand what would and would not happen next. There would be no surgery. The standard protocol required chemotherapy and radiation first. Surgery only happened if those didn't eliminate the cancer completely. Because of the potential harm to the sphincter muscle, surgery was a last resort. He would now step out of the picture until after I'd completed treatment, so it was time for me to move to the next phase. He sent me home with instructions to immediately make an appointment with an oncologist. In response to my request for a referral, he gave me one name to start with—an oncologist whose office was close to where we live. He wasn't certain, though, whether that oncologist treated anal cancer. The next steps of this journey had been defined: find an oncologist and get going with treatment.

The irony of what lay ahead did not escape me. I now had to face the modalities I'd been able to avoid with breast cancer. I was about to undergo the treatments that represented two of my biggest fears. Could I not only face them but embrace them?

Irony or Opportunity?

I t was impossible to ignore the significance of my current situation with regard to treatment options. I couldn't help but think back to my time at the Chopra Center. When I left the center, after conversations with Dr. David Simon and his colleague, as well as after reading his book *A Return to Wholeness*, I was ready to *take it all* if necessary, including chemotherapy and radiation. I planned to have a mastectomy, but if anything showed up in my lymph nodes, I intended to do whatever it took to eliminate the cancer. I surrendered and came to accept that I would undergo whatever course of treatment was required. I have to admit, though, that when I learned I would not need any post-surgical treatment, I was not only relieved, but I was elated. As prepared as I had been to take on "all of it," not having to surrender to a subsequent course of treatment was the biggest gift I could have received at the time, and I was extremely grateful.

Anal cancer was different. I had to come to terms with the knowledge that I would undergo both chemotherapy and radiation, and the chemotherapy drugs that would be used were two of the "big hitters." I didn't know this early on but eventually learned about the drugs' significance during my first hospitalization.

This was a big ask of me from the Universe—to face what not only caused me intense anxiety but evoked terror. Until the moment I heard the prescribed treatment, I had no idea that I was *that afraid.* I would now have to face and embrace what I considered my most frightening adversaries, almost more fear-inducing than the cancer itself. As much as I wanted to be a big, brave Amazon woman and be able to say that this experience presented me with an opportunity to learn and grow and be healed, I couldn't help but admit that I was scared to death.

Are You My Doctor?

J ust like in Dr. Seuss's book *Are You My Mother?* I began to search for my oncologist. I knew this person needed to have experience treating this type of cancer, but there was more to consider. They needed a compassionate bedside manner, the ability to make me feel I had 100 percent of their attention when we were together, and to convey a sense of understanding that we were a team.

I soon learned that the protocol was standard—they all followed the same regimen for anal cancer. Within that prescribed protocol, however, I wanted someone who would see me as an individual with my own personality, needs, and viewpoints. I wasn't looking for someone to modify the protocol—I now understood that I was at an age and dealing with a type of cancer where I couldn't delay unnecessarily or bargain with what needed to be done. I also understood that the protocol they would follow was the best that Western medicine had to offer at the time, with studies showing a significant success rate and the complete elimination of cancer in most cases. I had to trust in science this time. What I needed was someone who would consider my thoughts and feelings and experiences along the way. Little did I know just how important that would turn out to be!

I wanted to work with someone who would truly be able to see that they were treating Donna Mazzitelli. And if they had a spiritual sense, that would be even better. Not religious, but spiritual. Since I would be putting my life and well-being in their hands, I needed someone who understood and acknowledged the awesome responsibility and profound sacredness of their role with regard to my life and longevity.

When I called the office of the oncologist my surgeon had told me about, I learned that he dealt primarily with breast cancer patients. I could have worked with him but decided I wanted to find someone with more experience in other areas. I found two other doctors in two different medical groups who seemed to have extensive experience with rectal, colon, and anal cancers. They happened to both be women. They were both specialized and had gone to great schools. One of them had a secondary degree in divinity. I was intrigued. I called their offices and scheduled appointments. The first was booked out for almost two months but just so happened to have a cancellation the following week. I took the appointment. I was then able to schedule an appointment with the second doctor for the very same day. Divine synchronicity—the significance of "appointment day" did not escape me. I supplied them with copies of my records in advance of our appointments. It seemed that everything was falling into place.

Both women turned out to be equally competent. They were informative and knowledgeable. They approached our first appointment in different fashions, yet they both covered the same elements—gathering information from me and describing how they would approach my treatment. The first doctor advised me that we should delay our trip to Europe and start treatment as soon as possible, an initial chunk of disappointing news to digest. I'd hoped to stall long enough so we could go away and celebrate our anniversary first, yet that was still about a month away.

We saw the second doctor at the end of her day, and she was running an hour behind by the time she stepped into the room. Dominic and I assumed she would whisk us in and out once we got into the exam office. To our surprise, she approached the appointment as if it were nine in the morning rather than six at night, and she spent the next hour with us. She also said she believed we should start treatment as soon as possible but understood that it would be our decision ultimately.

Clearly, choosing my doctor was tough. As Dominic and I reviewed our time with each woman, we could find nothing negative about either one. It was going to come down to my personal preference. Dominic said he'd be comfortable with either one. They were both extremely knowledgeable and seemed to offer a calm, confident bedside manner. *How do I decide?* I wondered. *How do I choose?*

Janet suggested a process to help me figure it out. The process involved asking specific questions of different parts of myself in order to come to consensus, using the blueprint of a square as the tool. In each corner of the square was a different part of me: body, mind, essence, and life force. At the center was the honoring of the entirety of *me*.

To use the tool, I needed to ask a question, the same question, to each part. My question was: How do I decide which doctor to work with?

My body answered, "Go with your gut feeling. Feel into who you connect with."

My mind answered, "Choose the one who seems honest, positive, forward-moving, and is a confidence-building person."

My essence answered, "Go with the one who will offer you support so you don't decide to check out from life during the process ahead. Someone who will inspire you to hang in there, who can hold an anchor to support you staying on the planet. You're looking for a spiritual partnership."

My life force answered, "You are looking for the one who will tend the fire and who sees the sacred responsibility of her role."

My center answered, "It is the one who will *honor You!*"

Because of what my life force, essence, and center indicated, I knew who I had to choose. It was the oncologist who had integrated the study of divinity with her medical degree. Not only was that on her CV, but she exuded compassion and a sense that we would go through this together. Not because she had to take on my cancer, not because she would discount her knowledge or expertise, but I had the sense that with her, *we* would work together to restore *me* to health. We were going for *cure*, and she even spoke of that.

When we met for the second time, I told her that I needed her to understand we would be in a sacred partnership and that I needed to work with someone who understood that. As she responded, looking directly into my eyes with deep compassion, it was apparent that she did: "Yes, we will be working together to get through this," she stated. "You have a very long life ahead of you."

Anyone can follow a protocol, but not everyone can honor the individual patient and their unique circumstances. It was clear to me that she would do both. I was in good hands. I'd found my sacred union and knew I was home.

Why Is This Happening?

After the surgeon's initial conclusion that I had a cancerous tumor, and prior to the colonoscopy and biopsy he performed, fear and anger emerged once more. *How can this be happening? Why now? Why me? Why again?* Unable to sleep, I awoke at night and turned over these questions in my mind. *Dominic and I just found our way back to each other, and now I have cancer? Again? How can this be? I've worked hard to deepen my spiritual life. I faced my part in the demise of our marriage. I've forgiven so much in my life. I've tried to live in healthier ways physically ... but maybe I really haven't ...*

Is it because I haven't been exercising? Is it because I let my diet slip—I've gone back to consuming sugar and white flour and coffee and eating meat? Is it because I did something wrong? Am I being punished? Did I screw up? Did I not do

*enough or change enough? Did I do too much? Did I allow too
many things to happen that hurt me? Why is this happening?*

After the colonoscopy and as I looked for my oncologist, more
questions and thoughts woke me during the night. *Why is this
happening to me?* I asked over and over again. *What do I need
to learn? What do I need to do differently? Am I going to make
it through this? Will I live to see my girls become truly independent and self-sufficient? Will I see them find joy and happiness
in their lives? Will I see them begin to heal from the decisions
they've made in recent years that have caused them intense suffering? Will I live to see their children? Why the fuck is this
happening now? What did I do wrong?*

I couldn't seem to stop blaming myself for what was happening to me. In my journal on February 15, the day after I got the
pronouncement of cancer, on Dominic's birthday, I wrote, "I'm
beating myself up today. If only … I went to the doctor sooner.
If only … I didn't try to ignore what was happening. If only …
I avoided thinking this could be serious. If only. Now I sit here
with the words spoken by the colorectal surgeon yesterday: 'This
isn't good. I don't like this. I believe it's cancer.' I'm trying to stay
positive, but what does that mean?"

The surgeon said my delay hadn't made the situation worse.
He was certain of that. Yet, I couldn't help chastising myself for
not going sooner. Even though I'd been misdiagnosed at the ER, I
blamed myself. Then I questioned why I had cancer again. *What
did I do wrong? What did I miss? What didn't I learn the first
time? Did I ask for this? Did I manifest this myself for me to learn
something?* My thoughts got more and more twisted and confused.

In the end, after so many nights of turning these questions over and over, the question that had begun as "Why me?" became "Why not?" and "Why not me?" I was not any more special than anyone else. And in the end, it didn't matter why it was happening. What truly mattered was what I would do about it and how I would handle the journey ahead. The answer to that is splashed throughout my journal.

I desired more than anything else to handle the journey ahead with grace and ease. So that was where I needed to begin. No more looking back. It was now time to look at what was happening and begin to address it, deal with it, and experience it with as much grace and ease as I could muster. Now was the time to be fully present to what was happening in my life. "Grace and ease, grace and ease, grace and ease" became my daily mantra. It was truly the only possible answer to "Why is this happening?"

Cancer returned in February.
A new expression of her.
Another pronouncement on Valentine's Day.
"Will you listen now?" she asked.
"There is more for you to understand.
This is a time of refinement.
Embrace me. Embrace You. This won't take long.
I believe you're ready to let it all go."

A Conversation with the Unexpected Inhabitant

The unexpected inhabitant returned once more on Valentine's Day.

"Go deeper," she said. "I am here to teach you. There is more for you to learn."

"But I thought you taught me everything last time. I thought I learned what I needed."

"Refinement," Cancer replied. "This is a time to refine."

"What did I miss? Why? Why now? Why me? Why anal cancer? I don't understand."

"You've done nothing wrong. You missed nothing. You faced what you were ready to look at. You've grown, you've opened yourself to experience more of life—to love, to forgive, to have compassion for others."

"So why are you here?" I asked.

"Because you weren't ready then, but you are ready now."

"For what?"

"Deep down, in the darkest recesses of you, in the caverns you avoid, lie fear and shame and grief. You try to ignore these places; you strive to deny their existence. But they are there. They've been there for a long time. It's time to release them. It's time to forgive, to love, and to have compassion for yourself."

"How do I do that? Where do I begin?" I asked.

"With me. I am here to help you begin. Together, if you are willing, we will bring forth and release the pain that still clings to you. I am here to work with you if you will allow me."

"How do we begin?"

"By letting me show you the way back. Back to what it means to truly believe that the most important being is you. It all starts and ends with YOU!"

In that moment, I knew this was no foe to be feared. This was no evil sorcerer to be battled. I looked into the eyes of Cancer. What was there was pure Divine Love. What emanated was compassion for all I'd experienced and for the many ways I'd hurt the most important person in my life—ME.

Who stood before me was a friend, and I was ready to walk with her to the shore's edge, where I knew in my heart we would part ways. Until then, we would journey together and get to know each other.

"Thank you, friend. I'm ready."

Unwanted Guests

After seeing the oncologists and the surgeon, my path was clear. Chemo and radiation would be the treatments for this cancer. No surgery, at least not initially, and probably not ever. Chemo and radiation … the two approaches that still scared the hell out of me. The two unwanted guests to deal with the uninvited inhabitant—these unplanned occupants and unexpected visitors.

I wrote in my journal on February 24, the day I saw the surgeon for my biopsy results: "How do I allow them to enter me in a hospitable way? How do I greet them and even thank them for coming? We would never invite a guest into our home who we thought would hurt us, so how do I do this? I would never purposely put poison in my body unless I wanted to harm myself. So how do I do this? How do I become gracious and allow for this lengthy visit with grace and ease? I'm not sure right now."

Two days later, as I sat quietly with one of my spiritual tools, a message from the Divine came to me:

"Be grateful for ALL of it."

Lotus flower—white with a yellow throat, appeared in my mind's eye to reinforce the message.

"Be grateful!"

On February 28, I received a second message. This time, only words:

"Keep listening in the moment.

When fear comes up, return to flow.

Let yourself be loved.

Use your support.

You are important!

Use me to bring you to flow. Use Me!"

Each morning over the coming weeks, I sat quietly with the same spiritual tool.

On March 3, I heard:

"No pushing.

No pulling.

No stopping, blocking, or resisting.

Just allow all to unfold and flow.

You are being supported."

On March 8, I heard:

"Listen to the birds—listen.

Look upon nature.

Be here now!

Sit on the sand and let the beach soothe you.

Pull from memories of nature when needed."

Although I sat in my chair looking at the Colorado mountains, I could close my eyes and be in Hawaii or on a California beach. I could travel to Florida. I could sit in a forest of redwoods or by a Monterey cypress or under a palm tree in Kauai. I could hear the rustle of leaves and branches or the in-and-out rhythm as the waves rolled onto the shore and receded. The Divine was showing me the way.

As I faced decisions regarding timing and the beginning of this journey, I saw that not only would I entertain these uninvited guests, but I would also be graced with the presence of majesty and beauty beyond my wildest expectations. Along with the unexpected and the unwanted would be the blessed support of the unseen.

In this merging, in this flow, grace and ease would be there. I truly would be held and uplifted. I was not alone. All I had to do was listen and look. More support than I ever dreamed possible would take this journey with me. Even more than I understood.

Words

As much as I had begun to open myself to what I was about to undergo, and as committed as I was to moving through this experience with grace and ease, there were times when I reacted with anger and frustration at our medical establishment. On one particular morning, I began to journal about my agitation at the labels used—that we've bought into as a society.

"How does the medical community come up with the names they use? Who decides on the choice of words and phrases to label people's physical conditions? Incontinence, penile dysfunction, erectile dysfunction, incompetent cervix? Viable pregnancy, geriatric pregnancy, and so many more descriptions that make a person feel 'less than,' leaving an individual with the belief that their body has betrayed and failed them. We can begin to feel as badly about ourselves because of the label as we do about the condition.

"Yet, when it comes to the battery of tests required to make a diagnosis, they create *cute* acronyms, benign names, most likely to make us feel better about what we are undergoing. 'You need a PET scan.' 'We've ordered a CAT scan.' Adorable, aren't they? Although significant and notable in our current array of diagnostic tools, the acronyms help us forget that to obtain the information necessary to make a diagnosis, we must ingest, be injected with, or be bombarded with radioactive materials that light up our internal landscape. And there's absolutely nothing *cute* about that.

"I wonder when the time will come that our diagnostic tools and treatments will have less potential to cause further harm. I wonder when the words used to describe one's medical condition will offer hope and encouragement for the healing of our bodies. I wonder when those words will provide the neutrality necessary to see the amazing resilience and the mechanisms of healing that our bodies are capable of doing without even trying. I wonder."

The following morning, I continued journaling right where I left off. Apparently, more needed to come up and out, more needed to be expressed. I was searching to find a more loving and hopeful way to speak about our illnesses and the way we deal with them. I was desperate to find a way to focus on healing and surrender rather than on disease and fighting.

"And what about the words we use when dealing with a disease or life-threatening medical condition? How many of us have heard the phrases and words meant to encourage?

"'You must fight.' 'He needs to fight.' 'She isn't fighting hard enough.' Not only are we told to fight, but we're reminded that this is a battle, maybe even the biggest battle of one's life. And when someone isn't doing well physically or is too tired to undergo further treatment or is ready to let go of their life, they're told to fight harder. They're reminded that they can 'beat this,' if only they'll keep fighting. They're *encouraged* to think that they can win this battle—they just need to *do more*. It's all about fighting and pushing and being stronger than whatever they're dealing with. Above all else, they cannot give up.

"When someone lies dying, we sometimes become angry, believing that they gave up and didn't try hard enough. Once more, the message is that the person is doing something wrong. And when someone passes, we sometimes use expressions such as 'The cancer took him' and 'The cancer was too strong for her to beat.' We become angry at the disease and angry at the person. We wish they had done more to save themself.

"Surrender cannot be part of one's vocabulary because that represents giving in, and the person cannot give in, no matter what. Acceptance and surrender are seen as weaknesses—they represent giving up, acquiescing, and not trying hard enough. They're seen as complacency.

"All of this implies there is an entity to fear and fight—an enemy to neutralize, a foe to destroy. These words and phrases invoke images of bad guys to take down and rip apart. But what we fight only grows stronger. What we battle implies that we are a victim.

"When we 'beat the opponent,' we're labeled a survivor. We join walks and runs and don shirts that mark us as the survivors or connected to one. We vow to raise money to fight harder, to bring awareness to the enemy that must be conquered. 'We will never surrender,' we vow. We focus on the illness. We don't want to forget its name. We create awareness days to emphasize the disease—as if anyone can ever forget that diseases like cancer exist. But rather than Ovarian Cancer Awareness month or Breast Cancer Awareness month, what might it look like for us to refer to September and October as Ovarian Health Awareness month and Breast Health Awareness month? Why not focus on our health and encourage women to get screenings to stay healthy rather than frighten women into compliance to make sure there is no cancer lying in wait in our bodies?

"The words we choose are extremely important. They conjure images. They create stories. They can elicit fear or offer support and encouragement. In the case of cancer, they can also elicit impressions of right and wrong, winners and losers, good guys and bad guys. They can amplify the need to resist and oppose, to even attack. But who do we attack? Who do we fight? What are we resisting?

"These cells that mutated within my body are mine—they always were. The tumor that formed is a part of me—it always was. Not always in the shape and form of a mass, but the potential was always there. When I fight it, I battle myself—my own body. When I resist, I go against me. Yet, when I accept, I embrace all of me rather than only certain parts, rather than only what I like or what is easy to accept and be with.

"Seeing a perceived foe as a friend is where the real understanding begins. That's where learning and insights are possible. Whether that friend is with me for a day, a year, or the rest of my life, this is the time when I get to know and love myself in my entirety. And that's when the real healing happens.

"I look forward to the day when we are no longer told and encouraged to battle and fight. Instead, let us accept and understand and love our way back to wholeness and perfect health.

"It's all in the words we tell ourselves—and the words we express to others. It starts with the words. Will our words encourage understanding and truth? Will they be founded in reality? Or will they foster illusion, mistrust, and self-doubt? Today, I vow to choose my words wisely."

My journal reflected an impassioned plea for societal change to bring healing and hope to as many people as possible. However, as I reread what I'd written over those two days, I realized my words were meant for me. To come to my truths. To create language and definitions that fit me. To redefine my approach for moving forward. All from a place of surrender. All with grace and ease.

More Ink

The day I went in for my initial radiation appointment, I
didn't know what to expect. I was told I'd see the doctor
and two of my nurses and then have a scan performed
by a tech. They needed to get precise measurements of the tumor's
location in order to decide where to focus the radiation. I expected
that they would focus the radiation beam on the tumor directly,
but that wasn't the case. They would use the arc method, which
meant the beams would be arced around my body—first the front
and then the back—sweeping around to ensure that my entire core
body was "hit." More rads of radiation would be concentrated on
my left side, the side where the tumor was located, but my entire
lower body would receive the radiation treatment.

Once he looked at the images, the radiation oncologist determined that I would receive thirty-three treatments. They would

be done five days a week, Monday through Friday, over a six-and-a-half-week period. The process and duration were huge pieces of information to ingest and digest. A large percentage of me would be radiated. I would later learn that radiation will never again be a treatment option in that part of my body since I'd received the maximum allowed for my entire lifetime. At that time, all I knew was that my body would be receiving treatment in a far greater scope than what I'd imagined. Until this procedure and the process were explained to me, I'd naively thought a beam could be directed at the tumor, focusing exclusively on its eradication. It came as quite a shock to realize how "off" my imaginings had been.

After the two-month plan was laid out for me, the next step was for the tech to mark my body at the three places that would be "lined up" each time I came in for treatment—one on each hip and one at my pubic bone. To mark them, I would receive a permanent dot at each spot. I'd had plans for my second tattoo, but this was not what I'd envisioned, I told the tech. We laughed—I, a little nervously. She took her inking gun and shot ink into each spot. Within minutes, it was done—three black marks—each no bigger than a pin head, were embedded into my skin.

She and I then set up the appointments—thirty-three times I'd come in for radiation, along with a scheduled massage at every fifth treatment. Although I'd just learned the scope of the radiation treatment, it still sounded doable to me. Denial was helping me cope for the time being.

The most difficult piece of information came at the end of my appointment with the tech. My first radiation treatment was set for March 24, eleven days later, and two days before our thirty-first wedding anniversary, the anniversary we'd planned to spend in Paris and London. To avoid the risk of having my tumor continue to grow or to have the cancer begin to spread, there would be no travel in the near future. I'd already agreed that we needed to start treatment as soon as possible, yet the reality of my start date hit hard.

Trying to keep my emotions in check, I reminded myself it was the right thing to do. As much as I wanted to celebrate our marriage and reunion with Dominic, and as sad as I felt about having to postpone, I knew that the cloud hanging over both our heads would be a deterrent to a true celebration. I understood it was best to wait for a happier and healthier time to go on our special trip.

I moved to the next phase of my appointment—a meeting with one of the nurses to go over what to expect during my treatment. She described the changes that radiation would cause to my skin, as well as internal changes, especially diarrhea. She sent me home with a plastic tub to use for sitz baths, Aquaphor to apply to my skin, and my promise that I'd let them know if I needed anything else.

The second nurse came up and hugged me as I was about to leave. "You are our heroes," she said. "You are all so brave." I smiled with tears in my eyes at her kindness. I didn't feel like anyone's hero, though, nor did I want to be one. Although the first nurse had informed me what to have on hand, including unscented baby wipes to use instead of toilet paper, I still couldn't get my head around what was coming. I had no frame of reference for this experience. I left wondering if they were all making a bigger deal about the treatment than it actually would be. I'd soon come to know that it could be everything they said and more.

Purple Power

The day my port was surgically implanted, it all began to hit me even harder. *This is really happening! I'm going to have chemo. Just like Dad did for so long, I'm going to be infused with this poison. I now have a port just like he did.*

But unlike my father was able to do, I knew with complete certainty that I would live beyond sixty-seven years old. *I want to live to a very old age. One hundred and five is my magic number. Has been and still is! So suck it up, and let's get through this!*

My oncologist said they'd watch closely for infection and fevers. They'd watch for my need to get built up with injections to increase my white count. I remembered how my dad received injections to build his red count at the same time as one of our infant daughters received them while in the NICU. All of the issues my oncologist said they'd watch for and address if and when they happened triggered more fear and vivid memories of my father: his weight loss, his pale skin, his hair loss, his exhaustion. Yet, through it all, he never lost his sense of humor or his smile. They helped him deal with everything he was experiencing. He hadn't been much older than I when he started treatment. He had been sixty-two years old—I was now fifty-eight. Young. We were both young.

When the port was being put in, I decided to smile, just as I knew my dad had done. The doctor came to see me before we got started. He said he'd had a port—he'd been through treatment himself. He told me that the best day was when they removed it, and he promised that day would come for me too. The port was a Power Port—"Purple Power," they called it. They even had a purple plastic bracelet you could wear that said "purple power." In an emergency, it would notify first responders that I had a port inserted. I chose not to wear it, but I did need to carry a card that said I'd had one put in on March 14, 2014.

The most important assurance I needed before they inserted the port was that my tattoo would not be damaged since the port and my tattoo were on the right side of my chest. Everyone fell in love with my tattoo, and it became the center of conversation. It made everyone smile and ooh and ahh, just as the team responded when I had my colonoscopy. My monarch butterfly, lotus flower, and black panther would be unharmed, they assured me. A nurse asked the meaning, and I told the story of how the images came to be. Maybe I'd get another tattoo to commemorate the completion of this process, I told them.

Before I knew it, my port was installed. We'd laughed and smiled and chatted the whole way through.

"When you come back the next time we see you, you'll get it removed, and we'll give you a giant cookie to celebrate. We all celebrate when our patients' ports are removed," my doctor said with a big smile.

Yes, we'll celebrate, I thought. *I will welcome that day. For now, though, it's time to heal for two weeks before the chemo begins.*

Hit by a Train

Yes, the day my port went in, I could no longer deny what lay ahead. "I am going to receive chemo," I said out loud to no one in particular. I couldn't deny that creating an opening for chemo to be infused scared the hell out of me. I was allowing an entry point for the poison I'd vowed never to permit into my body.

After the procedure, when they handed me all the literature and paraphernalia that went with my "Purple Power" port, they also pointed out the spill kit included in my "New Patient Kit." Containing gloves and an OSHA-approved yellow biohazard bag, along with an 800 number to call in the event of a spill, I needed to take this home and have it available. I'd be on a pump receiving chemotherapy in five-day increments. Over two five-day periods, the pump would continuously infuse chemo into my body. The spill kit was provided in case anything detached. The spilled chemo would need to be cleaned up using a precise protocol to avoid harming myself and others.

Once more, I couldn't deny the severity of what I was about to undergo. I would have two weeks to get my head around this. Time for the port to heal into my body. Time to accept the path ahead. The latter would be tougher to achieve in two weeks' time.

After having done everything necessary to begin treatment, all I could do was wait for the day my chemo and radiation treatments would begin: March 24. With each passing day, my anxiety grew.

In an attempt to minimize the fear growing inside me, I did what I could to prepare. I recorded meditations and visualizations from David Simon's book *Return to Wholeness*. I got essential oils ready and made sure my recorded music contained works that would help me create a sense of calm. I shopped for comfortable clothes to wear to each day's treatment, athletic attire that would look nice and be easy to slip on and off. All was coming together. Dominic and I planned possible food options—meals and snacks I'd hopefully be able to tolerate. We got prescriptions filled in anticipation of nausea and the changes to my skin. All needs were being addressed internally and externally. All, that is, except my growing sense of dread.

"This is like standing on the train tracks as you watch the train coming closer and closer. It's like standing there and letting the train hit you," Janet said with deep compassion for my state of mind. "I wish we knew someone who was a trained Navy Seal," she continued. "They are trained mentally to deal with things a normal human being would never conceive of dealing with."

"I wish I knew someone like that to talk to," I replied. Then it hit me. Dominic had trained hundreds of students to fly IFR, teaching them to ignore what was outside the cockpit window and trust their instruments. I had sat in the backseat more than once as a student was being taught how to focus on their instrumentation and take their cues exclusively from that information.

"Dominic can help," I replied. I then told her all about what I had seen and heard him teach in the long-ago past.

"Perfect! Go home and sit down with him and have him help you understand how a person learns to do what the mind normally doesn't want it to do, how to override what your mind is telling you to do."

Relieved to have a plan, I left our meeting. Having a task to focus on would help me cope in the remaining days before treatment was to begin.

Power and Performance

After meeting with my mentor, I went home and, to Dominic's surprise, asked him to help me understand how a person gets their mind wrapped around instrument flying, relying on their instrumentation rather than what they think they see outside the cockpit window.

He explained to me how certain instruments are related to power and others are related to performance. He also explained that when flying without reference to the horizon, one needs to rely on their instrumentation. What one needs to avoid is using the visuals outside the cockpit window since in instrument flying, the horizon disappears.

As he went through each instrument and its purpose, I began to consider how this related to the flight I was about to embark upon. I was most definitely about to take off into the clouds without any sense of the horizon. My destination was the elimination of cancer and restoration of my health, but the flying conditions I would encounter were yet unknown. From everything I'd been told and from what I'd witnessed in my life, it would get bumpy.

"Ninety percent of the time, a pilot focuses on her attitude indicator. The other 10 percent of the time, she scans her supporting instruments," he explained.

Number one was attitude—whether your plane is going up or down or right or left. I saw the correlation. What would be my attitude moving forward? It was clear that this would be my primary flight instrument. How would I see the process ahead? Would I interpret what happens going forward as making progress or experiencing setbacks? Would my mind maintain the attitude to keep me in the air? What about my emotions? Would I plummet to the depths of despair, or would I be able to stay the course—accepting the ups and downs, veering away at times, but still able to maintain forward movement? And how would I perceive the chemo and radiation I was about to receive? Would I fight against them, thinking they were causing me further harm, or would I be able to see that they were here to save my life? This seemed most important of all—my attitude about the treatment going into my body.

One by one, I considered each of the supporting instruments and how they related to the journey ahead. The next was the airspeed indicator, which sits to the left of the attitude indicator. What would be the speed of this process? What would be the speed of the release of cancer, and what would be the speed of my recovery and my ability to re-enter my life and my work?

To the right of the attitude indicator is the altimeter. Would I be able to stay above the fear related to my views of chemo and radiation? Would I be able to stay above the drama related to our daughters, who were each in the midst of their individual struggles? Would I be able to stay in the "range" necessary to ensure my regained health?

Dominic talked about each instrument one by one before reiterating, "So, the instrument a pilot focuses on primarily is the attitude indicator. It gives you a two-dimensional view of the aircraft's relative position to the horizon. She relies on the attitude indicator to keep her flying straight and level and scans the other five supporting instruments as needed to make further corrections." It made sense. My attitude would be, and need to remain, my number one focus. Everything else would give me additional information related to what might be impacting and affecting my attitude.

I saw the questions these instruments help to answer regarding performance: Is the process too slow or too fast, am I banking too steep, am I heading in the right direction? What would be my body's overall performance, and how might I support it? But what about the power required to make it through? What would I need to manage the situation and have the power necessary for my body to perform well under such adverse conditions? Like flying through a thunderstorm (which pilots do everything possible to circumnavigate), chemo and radiation would bombard my body, sending shockwaves and liquid lightning into every cell. Since I couldn't avoid this storm, would I be able to manage it and stay on track?

This would not be an easy flight or a short one. If I believed what the nurses had described, I would be taking a treacherous journey filled with perilous, even life-threatening, conditions. They'd instructed me to purchase supplies to make me more comfortable, but I needed a resource that went beyond trying to manage the physical challenges.

I would need a visual to focus on, just as a pilot focuses on her instruments when flying in the clouds—a visual to give me courage and strength for the journey ahead, to remind me that I had support to help me navigate this unfamiliar and frightening territory. With Janet's help, I identified that I needed a bowl, a container, where I could put items that would help me focus. Dominic and I went to a home store, and I found the perfect receptacle—a white, oval-shaped bowl with two handles.

With white ribbon, I tied bright cotton-candy-pink hearts to each handle. One heart said "power," and the other said "performance." Inside the bowl, I put the visual of the cockpit along with other items that would bring a smile to my face and remind me that I could get through this—that a better life was waiting for me once I landed.

Just like my body would be purified and cleansed and cleared, this bowl signified the possibility of all I would ultimately put into my body and the tools I needed to remain in flight. Beyond that, the love, dedication, and devotion being showered on me from my family and close friends, and most especially from Dominic, would be a source of strength and a place to focus. With these physical reminders of the power available to me and the potential for my body to make it through this storm, I was finally ready.

The Five
Stages of Hair Loss

hen I initially met with the oncologist I'd chosen, she went over the bodily side effects I would experience. They included mouth sores and changes to my nails, as well as digestive changes. Dehydration could become an issue. Infections and fever were big concerns, so they would watch for them along with drops in my white cell counts, which were highly probable.

This would not be an easy road. Although short in duration—six and a half weeks if everything could be done without any breaks in treatment—it would be intense. The first week would be continuous drip chemo delivered via a pump I would wear plus daily radiation, then three weeks of radiation only, followed by another week of continuous drip chemo and daily radiation once again. That would be followed by a final week and a half of daily radiation. If I could tolerate it—my body, that is—this would be the plan. This was the protocol for treating anal cancer: a concentrated effort.

One of the other side effects would be the loss of my hair, which she said would start to happen by the second week. In preparation for the inevitable, I decided to take matters into my own hands. My short hair had grown out some, and my gray roots were showing. Still caring about how I looked, I put into action my version of what I called "The Five Stages of Hair Loss":

1. *Denial. Color my hair solid brown—no more purple highlights that I'd been wearing for the past couple of years—and eliminate the gray roots. Make my hair all one color.*

I dyed my hair on a Saturday. Although my hair loss would happen, I chose to do what I could to make myself look good for a while longer. Maybe it was vanity, or maybe it was my need to feel normal for as long as I could. Probably it was a bit of both. I needed to feel like me for as long as possible.

2. *Anger. Cut my hair very, very short. Find a picture of a celebrity who wore it this way.*

I chose Alyssa Milano, who was wearing a pixie cut at the time. I got my hair cut the following day, on Sunday. I wasn't going to be robbed of my hair any sooner than necessary. So, along with a rich dark brown that was closest to my actual color, I decided to wear a pixie cut. The irony was that as a child, this cut had been imposed on me, and I'd hated it. Now I was choosing it for myself.

3. *Bargaining. Buy colorful scarves and funky hats. When my hair is gone, at least I will be able to look spunky.*

Dominic and I headed to two department stores, where I found fun, bright, and uplifting scarves—some made of cotton in more bold colors and others of blended materials in slightly muted tones—scarves that would match the colors and styles of whatever I wore. I've always looked good in hats and went through a time in the 1980s when I wore them almost daily, so I knew I could pull off hats as well. We found multiple styles and colors that made me excited about wearing them.

4. *Depression. Admit this is happening. With the results of the tests, the stage and grade of cancer had been identified and the treatment plan confirmed.*

These were the first moments when it became more real. Yes, this was cancer. Yes, it was stage 2. And yes, it was isolated in one tumor that consisted of squamous cells, the type related to anal cancer. The course of treatment was specific and clear—and there would be no surgery, unless cancer cells remained post-treatment. Hair loss was imminent.

5. *Acceptance. Buy an electric buzz-cut razor. Based on my doctor's prediction of when I'd begin to lose my hair, or based on when it began to fall out, shave my head. Actually, let Dominic shave it since he offered to do it for me.*

I didn't know exactly when I would do it, but I knew I definitely would. This was an element of what lay ahead that I could control—when I shaved my head. I acknowledged that I would lose my hair, but I didn't have to go through watching it fall out clump by clump, as I remember my father experiencing many years earlier. I remember what a difficult time he had as he grieved the loss of his handsome looks. Instead, I could shave my head and lose my hair with dignity and on my terms. Once more, it was about my willingness to allow the process to unfold to the best of my ability and to address what was happening with as much grace and ease as I could muster.

Visualization Meditation

The night before treatment was to begin, I couldn't sleep. No doubt about it: I was scared. The crushing waves of fear came in at full force. I'd gotten myself into a swirl over some information I'd read the previous week. All of a sudden, I doubted myself and my decision to follow the directions of my oncologists. I'd been instructed to stop taking supplements and told that I could not use them during treatment—antioxidants in particular. Suddenly, I was where I'd been in 2007—doubting my doctors, doubting the treatment, and doubting myself. *What the hell am I doing? What the fuck have I gotten myself into? What have I agreed to?*

I remembered what Janet had told me: "Remember your age, Donna. You have to acknowledge that your body at this age will not repair itself in the same way or at the same rate as it could when you were twenty, thirty, or even forty. It is not as forgiving of what happens to it as it once was. This is simply a truth of aging. And keep in mind that this is the best that modern medicine has to offer. Those who have created what is available to us are not out to kill us. That is not their intention. Right now, you need to take what modern medicine has to offer. Afterward, we can work to clean up and clear out what's been put in your body once you go through treatment. For now, though, you need to go through with it. You are needed on the planet. Your work is not done here, so you need to do whatever is necessary. The world needs you."

I tried to take comfort in her words. Although they were tough to swallow, I couldn't deny my reality. I was now in my late fifties. And the tumor was big enough that I could feel it. No meditation, no supplements, no energy work could take it away. I remembered what Dr. Simon had told me back in 2007: "If you were my wife, I'd march you to the hospital for whatever treatment was necessary. Ayurveda alone cannot cure our modern illnesses." It was time for me to accept this reality. I needed the help modern Western medicine could offer. And I needed to accept it with grace, ease, and a large dose of gratitude.

I finally got up from bed in the early morning hours before dawn and recorded three visualizations. They would help me focus on my health, my breathing, and a new way to view the chemo and radiation. Rather than as poison in my body, these two necessary treatments would help me let go of the tumor—allowing it to be carried away and returned to Universal Flow. In its place would come new cells—vibrant, alive, and whole. All that was attached to the tumor would be released with love and gratitude for what I could learn from it—if I was willing to embrace this tumor and the process.

I continued to sit in my bedroom chair, positioned by one of our bedroom windows so I could look toward the Rocky Mountains in the west. As the sun began to rise in the east, its light cast a glow on "Sleeping Indian," the majestic rock formation that greeted me each morning. Its grandiosity and solid strength told me there was nothing to fear. All in my path was there to be acknowledged and loved, embraced and released. I considered my body. The light—the beautiful rainbow light emanating from my heart space could fill my entire body, including the place where the tumor was. It could fill the darkness with light, releasing with love the cells that had lost their way in the process of gaining my attention. What could I learn from them, from this tumor, so that these out-of-control cells could leave and find their way back to the light?

The most essential message of all that came through in the early morning light was to love all of me, all of this tumor, all of this experience—to love the entirety of this experience. To love without shame or guilt or regret or judgment—and without anger. To love all parts of me—what I understood and what I didn't yet understand, what was easy to love and what made no sense to love. What was even difficult to love. The parts I hid away in shame, regret, and guilt. The parts I hid in remorse. The parts I was afraid to look at. I knew my tumor was all of those parts in one solid mass. Rather than being spread throughout my body, there it was, in one clump of cells begging for me to look within. Asking me

281

to stop being afraid to look back and to heal more of my past. In that moment, I found gratitude and a sense of relief, once more knowing this tumor was a friend who had come to show me the way to true love and compassion for myself, to learn to embrace and accept the ALL.

As difficult as it would be to look within, I could do it. And I could let go of this tumor and all it encapsulated. I wouldn't need to hold on to the tumor to understand what it represented. Everything I'd been afraid to acknowledge about my past—about what I'd experienced and what I'd created—was represented in this one big glob in a place in my body I couldn't actually physically get to. But I could feel this tumor. It had grown large enough that I could feel the physical pain of it, and I could see the effects of it in the toilet bowl—the shedding of blood, of my life force, that would continue unless I addressed it.

I knew what this tumor was asking of me—to feel, sense, and experience it—to be willing to begin the journey of looking at those parts of my life I'd kept hidden, or at least tried to keep hidden, from others. I didn't need to figure out everything before the tumor could go—I just needed to be willing to look at its deeper meaning, to commit to truly acknowledge and embrace all of the life I'd lived thus far.

After it was gone, even if it took many years, I could continue to do what was necessary to set myself free from the pain of my past. I could continue to work with what this tumor wanted me to look at. Now, though, through the process of my treatment, I could thank and release this *friend* back to Mother Earth and into Universal Flow.

As tears trickled down my cheeks, I looked out at the mountains once more. Knowing I wouldn't be alone physically or spiritually, I was ready. It was time to get showered. It was time to begin the work of healing and becoming whole.

Day One

Chemo and radiation began on a Monday. First stop: the lab. A fun and humorous nurse, Jean, did my blood draw. She explained everything as she went, making sure I understood why the various vials would be drawn and what they'd be monitoring as I progressed through treatment. She asked how I was doing, knowing this was Day One, and she acknowledged that being a bit scared goes with the territory. She assured me that everyone would help support me through this.

I was amazed when I found myself laughing and smiling in spite of how apprehensive I felt when I entered. Jean had a way of making it easy. Before I knew it, she'd accessed my port, drawn my blood, and had me ready to enter the infusion room. She walked Dominic and me in and introduced me to the nurses behind the desk. "I'm leaving you in good hands," she said with a smile before turning to go back to the lab. Soon enough, I learned just how true that statement was.

I made sure to leave my sarcastic, distrusting self at the door as we entered the infusion room—actually I hadn't even allowed her into the lab. I was learning.

Looking around, I saw nurses tending to patients—some obviously very sick—and two rooms with beds for patients who were unable to sit up in a recliner chair. One of the rooms was occupied. The door was ajar, and I could see a woman lying prone on the bed. I would eventually use that same room on more than one occasion.

A brown-haired nurse with a big smile told me to take a seat. She asked my name and said Erin would be over shortly. They'd been expecting me. Dominic and I found a patient chair in a quiet area at the center of the room with a guest chair next to it.

I felt inside my purse for my chemo-radiation bundle—the spiritual piece wrapped in fabric that I'd put together to walk with me through this journey. I touched my bottle of lavender essential oil, assuring myself that everything I needed to support me was close at hand. I could also feel the unseen—my guides, guardians, and mentors surrounding me—the ones I'd called on earlier that morning to be with me throughout this first day.

Erin came over to get things started. She asked if I'd like a warm blanket and showed Dominic where they were, explaining that we could grab as many as we wanted at any time. She showed us where snacks and drinks were. Everything we could want or need was there, including donuts and cookies on days when someone brought them in.

I tried to let go of my judgment about the kinds of "food" that were there, processed snacks filled with refined sugar and high fructose corn syrup—those "sugars" that cancer loves to feed on. I considered that once someone is here dealing with the effects of chemo, if a person can get a donut down their throat and hold it down, it's probably a good thing—a pleasure not to be denied or judged. Besides, the chemo was going to wipe out everything, so sugars were the least threatening substances in these rooms. Little did I know I would soon come to understand these thoughts more fully.

Once we were settled in, Erin checked in to see how I was doing. As she looked into my eyes with an expression of compassion on her face, it was obvious that she was inviting an honest answer, not some rote "fine" or "doing okay." She genuinely wanted to know how I was feeling and whether I had any questions or concerns I wanted to talk about before we began. Instead of standing over me, she sat next to me as she did her check-in and her assessment of my emotional state. I told her I was feeling both scared and sad. As she continued to sit beside me, she gave me a bit of time to be with my feelings, acknowledging that these were most definitely expected emotions. Then she stepped away to gather the supplies and medications we would need.

Erin explained everything we were doing as she proceeded. First, she inserted a syringe of saline directly into my port. This would always be done as a flush before and after anything else was inserted. Next came a syringe containing anti-nausea medicine and a steroid to help me tolerate the chemo. As she pushed it in, I saw that this cocktail was clear in color—*a neutral, non-descript liquid*, I thought. I didn't feel any fear or apprehension about it, only a sense of gratitude for how it would help me with what I knew was coming next.

The first chemo drug—mitomycin C—was light blue. *Madonna Blue. Just like the color often depicted for Mother Mary's mantle.* Although it was a smaller vial than the first two, it took longer to go in. Erin told me that it needed to be administered slowly and at a very specific rate. I held tight to my chemo/radiation bundle and tried to visualize Mary's help as I focused on what I'd brought along to support me.

Earlier, Erin had brought over a fanny pack for me—the pack I would wear home so that the five-day chemo drug would drip into my body at a consistent, round-the-clock rate. After she finished administering the mitomycin C, she went back to the medication room to prepare my next cocktail. I tried my best to continue to see these mixtures as the life-saving elixirs they were intended to be. It was still hard not to see them as poison, especially while looking at Erin and the other nurses, who all wore protective clothing and gear as they worked with patients. It was difficult not to acknowledge that they had to make sure they kept themselves safe from the drugs they were administering.

Erin returned a short time later and hooked me up to go home. Inside was 5FU (which I quickly began to call 5 Fuck You!—although I tried hard to let go of that name since I rarely used the "F" word). She set the rate of drip, and for the next five days, I would hear the rhythmic, consistent sound of the pump as it released chemo into my body, a sound I would come to have a love-hate relationship with.

Once everything was in place, we left and went to the hospital cafeteria for a cup of coffee before I had to be at my first radiation appointment. I immediately discovered that coffee didn't taste good—the effect of the chemo, at least the initial one, had already kicked in. *Wow! What else will change and how quickly?* I tried not to answer my own question by reviewing everything I'd been instructed to expect.

When we arrived in the radiation waiting room and took a seat, I looked across at a young woman with stubby hair. She was wearing a hospital gown wrapped around her with the opening at the front. I suspected she was there for breast cancer treatment. I'd been instructed that I would only have to pull down my pants and be draped with a sheet for my treatment. I'd have no need for their lockers and changing room or their hospital gowns. At the time, an easier process to get ready seemed to indicate an easier experience.

Within minutes, Paula, one of the two intake nurses, took me back to weigh me and take my vitals. She explained that once a week, I'd have this done. Additionally, I would see the radiation oncologist on that same day to monitor how I was doing—to check for how my body was tolerating the radiation and to evaluate the physical effects as we progressed. Paula warned me again that I would need to use all they'd given me during my initial appointment—the ointments, sitz bath, and baby wipes. All would be necessary, she reminded me. Again, I believed she was being overly cautious, maybe even exaggerating. Ultimately, I would need even more supplies—and even sooner than she'd prepared me for.

After my vitals and doctor visit, which focused on answering any remaining questions I might have on this first day, I returned to the waiting room. Within a few minutes, a tech came out to escort me to the radiation area.

As we entered the area where the massive radiation machine was located, we passed the control room, the place where the techs stay while a patient is being radiated. The two techs—one male and one female—introduced themselves. Carter and Suzie were gracious and friendly and did their best to assure me they'd be with me every step of this journey.

They explained that each day, they would take films before we proceeded with the radiation treatment. Those, along with my tattooed marks, would help them determine where they needed to focus the radiation beam.

It was time to begin. I lay down on the narrow sheet-covered "bed" (that was more like an extra-large, under-cushioned bench), and they draped me with a white sheet. As instructed, I pulled down my pants to just above my knees. Standing on either side of me, they lifted the bottom sheet to create a sling and adjusted my body according to where they believed I needed to be positioned. Then they left the room and took pictures from the control room. They came back, slid me a bit more, and then told me we were ready to go. As they returned to the control room and left me alone, I noticed music playing softly in the background. I tried to focus on the melody and lyrics.

Within seconds it seemed, the clicking and loud sounds of the machine and its movement told me we'd begun. *Lots of radiation*, I thought sadly. Another piece of this process that I needed to accept. As I lay there with my arms at my chest, holding my infusion fanny pack, I thought to myself: *This is it! We've really begun! There is definitely no going back now!*

I visualized rainbow light accompanying the radiation and wrapping my tumor in love. *Teach me what I need to learn, and then allow the rainbow light to escort you into Mother Earth's arms, where she can release you into Universal Flow. Thank you for being here. Rainbow light, would you be so kind as to embrace this tumor in your light and allow it to feel your love? I am ready to learn. I am ready to release this tumor into Universal Flow. I am ready to embrace this experience. I am scared, but I am ready.*

Soon enough, the machine stopped and the techs came back in. I was done for the day. Carter escorted me out to the waiting room where Dominic was sitting. I'd done it. "Congratulations," he said. "You did great!" Day One was complete.

Those Who Came Before Me

T hat first night, as I listened to the pump releasing chemo into my body, I thought of my father and Nonna. They had each suffered terribly with their cancers and the treatment of the times—my grandmother in the sixties and seventies and my father in the nineties. Although it seemed not much had changed regarding the available treatments, radiation and chemo had become more targeted and specialized since they underwent treatment. I didn't know what lay ahead for me, but somehow I sensed that my journey would be easier than either of theirs had been. I also knew without a shadow of a doubt that I'd survive, just as my mother had after undergoing a lumpectomy and radiation in 2006.

The radical mastectomy my grandmother underwent left her horribly disfigured. The outward scars and her dimpled chest reflected the barbaric surgery of the early 1960s—the hacking that was done in an attempt to remove all cancer. The radiation of the times also covered a much larger area of the body than the approach taken in the twenty-first century. All done in an attempt to eradicate what could not be detected with an X-ray. Years later, when the cancer returned within her body and on her skin, nothing could be done other than try to keep her comfortable. How much of the radiation she'd endured caused the cancer to literally pop out everywhere? I suspected it had a lot to do with her suffering in the early 1970s—and her ultimate death.

Yet, before she succumbed to the disease that encompassed her body internally and externally, she managed to attend her eldest grandson's wedding four months before she died. Attired in a beautifully simple dress in her favorite color red, with her hair coiffed and lipstick and blush applied, she beamed as she sat in her wheelchair, both at the church and at the reception that followed. Her dream of seeing at least one of her four grandchildren marry had come true.

When my father's non-Hodgkin's lymphoma returned as a huge lump on the side of his neck, it was time for him to undergo both radiation and chemo—the treatments his doctor had intentionally delayed more than twenty years earlier when he was first diagnosed. His doctor had wisely chosen to postpone any treatment and take a wait-and-see approach. For over two decades, my father's cancer had been in remission and completely disappeared. His doctor had warned him, though, once he determined that all his involved lymph nodes were not only back to normal size but did not indicate any signs of cancer: "Although we can now spread out your visits to once a year, don't forget that you are a ticking time bomb. Even though your case is one for the books, we don't know when or how the lymphoma will reappear, but it will come back. I am certain of that. As difficult as it is to say this to you, it will show up one day—we just don't know when that might happen or how it will present. In the meantime, go live your life."

My dad took his advice and not only lived, but he enjoyed life each and every day. He made sure that he and my mother traveled in the US and abroad, especially to Italy to see my mother's family, whom my dad adored, as well as to Hawaii, which was his favorite spot in the world. They even took trips to the East Coast, and he reconnected with his past and his remaining family in Pennsylvania, which allowed him to make peace with the horrid childhood he'd lived through.

His famous motto was "You can't take it with you," and he lived by it until the end. He never skimped on spoiling my mom with jewelry and clothing he knew she would never have bought for herself. They enjoyed dinner out with friends, musical theater and plays, and attended San Francisco 49ers games as season ticket holders during the reign of Bill Walsh, Joe Montana, and Steve Young.

Even in the last five years of his life, while undergoing radiation initially and subsequently ongoing chemo treatments, he participated and engaged in life fully. Twenty-two months before he died, he got himself and my mom to the hospital immediately following a chemo treatment so he could be there for the birth of our twins. He continued to work for a limo service and found ways to include a trip to see his granddaughters whenever possible. Until they were twenty-two months old, he made sure that not more than two weeks ever passed without spending time at our home with his "two girls."

I watched my father live joyfully and fully present until he couldn't anymore. He showed me that, although his treatment was extremely tough to deal with, and at least twice we almost lost him to complications from the chemo, he was determined to live life to the fullest. He was not about to let cancer or the treatment keep him away from what and who he loved. When he finally couldn't do it anymore, he let go and was gone within days.

Looking at pictures of him taken during those last two years, I see how much he was suffering and how badly the cancer and the treatment were ravaging his body. Yet, because of his spirit, it wasn't apparent to me at the time. For a long time, his internal desire to thrive in life overrode the outward appearance of his suffering.

Thinking about Nonna and my father, I considered that I'd been shown the way by two brave, courageous, and determined individuals who persevered well beyond what doctors believed was possible. Their internal spirits allowed them to live long enough to experience joys in their lives in the midst of their suffering. I could hear their words as I sat in my darkened living room.

"You've got this! You're brave too—I've watched you overcome extreme difficulties and find yourself in the midst of those challenges."

"*Brava, Donna. Mi bellissima bambina! Brava! Tutto coraggiosa! Sempre, tutto coraggiosa.*"

Focused on the two of them, sensing they were flanking me as my journey began, I knew I could do it too: I'd be as brave and courageous as they had been—as they believed me to be—and I'd do it with grace and as much ease as I could tap into.

The First Wall

By Wednesday, Day Three of my chemo and radiation treatments, things had changed. My butt hurt, I felt queasy, and food seemed to get stuck in my throat. Worst of all, my attitude had changed. Grace and ease and asking for support from all that was seen and unseen were replaced with fear, anxiety, and anger. I hated the sound of the infusion pump as it dripped chemo—5FU—into my veins. *5 fuck you!* I thought as I woke during the night on Tuesday to the pump's release of liquid poison. I felt trepidation every time I tried to think of the radiation as healing light. I tried, but I hurt physically and emotionally and couldn't deny that radiation was one of the culprits.

Feeling sorry for myself, at seven in the morning on Wednesday, I got out of bed. *Today is our wedding anniversary, and instead of being in Paris and London as planned, I have another day of treatment and feeling like shit ahead of me. This sucks.*

I listened two times each to the two visualization recordings I'd made. I knew my attitude was off. I tried to visualize the attitude indicator and focused on getting myself re-centered.

I knew I needed to focus on that attitude indicator. It was key. It was where I needed to rest my mind's eye rather than outside at all the exterior conditions. Yes, I hurt. Yes, I felt nauseous. Yes, I was scared and anxious. But focusing on keeping myself straight and level would and could get me through these turbulent conditions.

I asked out loud in the early morning quiet, "How do I adjust my attitude today? What do I need to keep me flying straight and level?" The answers came: "Smile! Feel gratitude that you're alive today! And let the tears come. Release them. They are there. Let them go!"

I wanted to be strong and thought my tears were a sign of weakness—an old pattern, a childhood message that still seemed to be running. Early in my life, I'd learned that crying left me ashamed. My uncle would laugh at me and call me the Daly City Waterworks (the city in California where we lived until I was six years old). Once we moved to Cupertino, I became the Cupertino Waterworks. I know he thought his humor would snap me out of my crying, but all his teasing did was make me feel embarrassed and ashamed and even afraid of him. He was a larger man than my father in both height and weight, and he had a big voice. As an Italian man, he had a huge presence. In actuality, he was more like a giant teddy bear than someone to be feared, but fear him, I did. Yes, he could get angry, but usually, he used humor and a bit of teasing to make his point. So Donna was the waterworks because she cried often, and he didn't want to see or hear me cry—I'm sure mostly because it made him uncomfortable.

Being called a crybaby at those times when I couldn't hold in my tears had added to my sense of embarrassment. Crying had been a release for me—until my tears became a source of ridicule and shame. In time, I rarely let tears flow. Instead, I stuffed down what I was feeling and tried to jump into action to find a way to solve whatever problem caused me to feel sad or hurt.

This time, though, I had no action to take. I had no way to escape what I was feeling, and I did not have the strength to fight against the rising emotion. "I can't help it," the voice of a much more recent part of me spoke up. "They are here, and I need to let them go!"

I'd forgotten how much tears allow for release and cleansing. In my struggle to keep steady, to act with grace and ease, I'd pushed down the healing emotion I needed to let flow. I finally gave in and cried. It wasn't a sobbing, body-shaking event but more of a gentle flow of the tears that I'd held back in the name of strength and courage. Being strong and courageous, I came to realize, didn't mean the absence of tears—it meant being present to everything I was experiencing.

Nausea kicked in more intensely as the day progressed and continued through the following weekend. Wednesday had been my hump day—the midpoint until the pump would be removed on Friday afternoon. Wednesday's symptoms kicked my butt. I wanted to rip out my IV. I fantasized about using the spill kit they had given me to clean up the mess once I yanked it out.

By the time I got to Day Three's radiation treatment, I could hardly tolerate it. I wanted to jump off the table and run. I wanted the day's treatment to be over within the first seconds it began. *How will I get through all thirty-three treatments,* I wondered, *if I can hardly face Day Three?* Every time the radiation machine made its noise and did another arc of my pelvis, I had to force myself to be accepting of its help. Admittedly, I wasn't doing well.

I received my first therapeutic massage after Wednesday's radiation session and felt the beginning of a shift. As this gentle, sensitive woman asked permission to touch me and found the places to allow her healing touch to enter me, tears streamed down the sides of my face. As I lay on my back and she massaged my upper shoulders and my arms, release came, and a wave of grace entered. With its gentle lapping, I felt ease. "Let go! Let go! Let go!" I heard. "Allow, breathe, release, breathe." With each gentle touch and stroke, I felt my anxiety subside. I felt my anger and fear dissipate. "You are loved!" I heard. "You are loved."

By Thursday morning, I entered the radiation room in a different space. Yes, I had shifted—my attitude was positive and optimistic once more. I felt calm and peaceful. I had a smile on my face. I was still nauseous, but I knew I could make it through the day and into Friday. My chemo week was more than halfway over, and I felt confident I could make it through the home stretch.

Usually, the music they played in the treatment room was barely audible over the loud clicking sounds of the radiation machine as it moved around my body. I smiled at Carter and asked, "Can you crank up the music louder today when I do my treatment?"

"Sure I can. We usually keep it low because patients want it that way. We can make sure it's up when you come in, and if I'm not here or if anyone forgets, just remind us. Any of us can do that for you."

"Okay. That sounds great. Thank you. I think the music will help me a lot as we go through the weeks ahead."

"Anything we can do to make this more comfortable, we're here for you."

"Thanks, Carter," I replied.

I could feel his kindness and compassionate understanding. All of the radiation techs had that gift, but he was definitely one of my two favorites.

After he got me set up, he left the room, and the music got louder. It filled the room with beautiful sounds—loud and clear over the noise of the machine as it started its daily journey around my body. As one familiar song morphed into another, tears began to run down my cheeks.

There are no accidents in life. Only messages to remind us that we are loved and supported always. As James Taylor sang to me, I knew I did indeed have a friend—even more than one.

Side Effects

On Thursday afternoon, I saw my nurse practitioner. I reported what I was experiencing. Nausea was on board now full-time. So was an increasingly raw and sore bottom. Diarrhea had also joined the party. Although none of this was easy, as I answered her questions, I felt a sense of ease. I would be free of the pump by Friday. Only one more day to go …

I went to radiation on Friday morning as the pump continued to administer chemo into my bloodstream. After my treatment, I checked the pump's display to see if anything had changed. The display and the pump's steady, rhythmic sound indicated it was still dispensing medication, just as it had for the past five days. *How long can it possibly take to release the rest of this? How far into today will this continue? Why is this going so damn slow?*

The morning seemed to drag on as I waited for the contents of the pump to empty. "A watched pot never boils!" I heard my mother say in my head. Of course, it doesn't!

I found myself getting more and more impatient. Why, I can't say. Nobody had promised it would stop in the early morning. Only that it would be sometime on Friday, most likely before noon. My appointment was set for 12:15 that afternoon, so it wasn't as if I could get unhooked any sooner anyway. I was just sick of listening to the sound of that pump. I wanted to hear a different sound: silence. My intolerance for the pump and the job it was doing had reached a crescendo.

At long last, I heard a new sound come from my pump—a two-tone beep. For a moment, I wasn't sure what it meant. *Check the pump. Maybe it's done.* I unzipped the black fanny pack and pulled out the pump. The words "reservoir volume empty" displayed across the LED screen. As the instruction sheet they'd given me explained, those words meant that "the medication was gone, and the pump had stopped." I was done! At least for the next three weeks, I would not have to listen to the sound of chemo's release into my bloodstream.

The chemo was all in, and so was I. No looking back, only moving forward. The liquid elixir was inside me and would do its magic within my body. I tried to see it as a healing potion rather than a poison. "It's the best that Western medicine has to offer, and you need it," I heard my mentor's words repeat in my head.

Yes, I need it. I can't do it alone. Grace and ease and gratitude. Ease and grace and gratitude. EGG! Accept. Allow.

Once I'd been unhooked by one of the chemo nurses and Dominic and I got in our car to head home, a sense of freedom washed over me. I felt lighter as I held the empty fanny pack on my lap. I knew I would need it again in a few weeks, but for now, I could set it aside on a shelf in my closet. I looked down at my chest. No tubing was connected to my port. Nothing had to be carefully tucked within my clothes and down to my waist. I was free! Having nothing attached to my body was exhilarating.

That thrill was short-lived, however. By 3:00 p.m., mouth sores began to pop out. Like having been scalded to the back of my throat, blisters suddenly appeared. They caused excruciating pain that made me wonder how I'd ever get anything down my throat again. In the beginning, I'd believed the nurses were exaggerating about side effects, but now I began to see and feel that they might have understated them. I hurt in my mouth, within my body, and on my butt. How would I ever get through this?

The Bridge

"I've got a homework assignment for you," Janet instructed. She'd called early in the morning to see how I was managing, sensing that I wasn't doing well physically or emotionally. "You've stepped onto the bridge, and there is no turning back. I want you to identify what's on that bridge with you."

"I get that I can't stop now, but you're saying there are things on a bridge to help me? I need to visualize the bridge and see what's there? That there's more supporting me than I'm aware of?"

"Yes," she replied. "And what I see there is amazing. The world needs you. Your work isn't done, and I see incredible support to take you through this," she added.

As much as I wanted to believe her, I still found it difficult at times to see my gifts and talents, to connect with the value of my life, to have faith in my purpose for being on the planet—and for staying on the planet and surviving this ordeal. But she was telling me that it was time to trust and believe in what was here to help me do just that. It was time to see what and who was there to support me; it was time to discover if I was willing to step onto that bridge.

Later that morning, I decided to try. I led myself into a meditation, and as I stepped onto the cobblestone path leading to the bridge, I heard and saw trolls to my left and right. They were positioned at the beginning of the bridge and below it. They stood there, not making any attempt to come at me or block my way. When I looked down as I stepped onto the wooden slats of the bridge, I saw dark, murky water below. Dense, dark fog enveloped me. *This is where I am right now*, I thought. *I don't know what lies ahead, and it's scary. I have horrible things to deal with, including the uncertainty of how this will all turn out. Will I even survive this?*

I grew quiet and allowed myself to move further onto the bridge. I remembered Janet's words that what is here is beautiful. *Let this scene unfold*, I instructed myself. *Don't give in to fear.*

I stood in this new spot and noticed what was happening. Light entered the fog, like a beam, from the other end of the bridge. I couldn't see the end, but I knew it was there. I felt presences on either side of me. Cautiously, I looked to my left and right. Giant white wings spread along the sides of the bridge and behind and ahead of me. They were preventing the trolls from climbing onto the bridge. *Archangels, they are archangels!* Massive, they expanded up into the sky, clearing my path so I could move forward.

I got to what I believed was the center of the bridge and felt my feet solidly rooted to the bridge's wooden planks. I felt stronger just standing there. More light seeped through the fog as if the fog was lightening up and beginning to lift. Then I began to see twinkling lights all around me, flitting and darting and bouncing. I felt a sense of gaiety, almost like I wanted to start giggling. *Fairies!* They surrounded me, bringing a sense of lightness with them, a sense of joy and calm. *Ease and grace, joy and gratitude,* I heard in my head. *They're helping me find it!*

I could see through the archangels' translucent wings to the water below. It was now bright blue. It glistened, and the water was clear. No longer murky or muddy. Ripples in the water expanded outward as if someone was dropping pebbles into it. People were now moving around on the bridge—laughing, playing, and dancing. Such joy! Such fun they were having! I looked ahead. Angels and light beings surrounded the most beautiful and bright rainbow I'd ever seen. The colors were glorious, the light iridescent. The angels and light beings flew and danced around as if they were dancing with the rainbow light.

I could see a clearing ahead filled with brilliant white light, the rainbow creating an archway through to the other side. I looked up and could see a full moon and light streaming down through the fog that was even brighter now. Moonbeams shot down to the ground. *So much light. So much color. So radiant,* I thought. I stood there, knowing it was not time for me to walk further. *Feel this. Bathe in it. Let it wash over and through you. Listen, breathe, feel.*

I stayed there for quite some time, basking in the light's energy and experiencing the love of all that was present until I felt full—completely infused with light and lightness. Then I opened my eyes and began to draw and write about all I'd just experienced.

"I saw them on the bridge this morning," I wrote. "All that are helping me. Wee people who are pushing my feet forward, fairies all around who are holding me up and helping me to continue moving, archangels who are using their wings to cut through the fog and keep the trolls away. A tunnel of light ahead being opened by more angels. I am being helped through this ordeal. I just have to not forget and to allow myself to feel their help. I am *not* alone, and I will be okay. Just keep moving forward and let them help!"

The previous night, I had hit a low point. I was angry. I hurt. I felt fear. I felt resentment. I felt frustration. I wanted it all to stop. To stop how I was feeling. To stop the treatment. To stop going for more hurt and more pain. I felt sorry for myself and wallowed in self-pity. But after doing as Janet had instructed and allowing myself to see beyond my physical limitations, I discovered I was not alone. I never had been.

"The fool is the one who believes only in what can be seen and felt on a physical level. The wise person is the one who allows their experiences to move into other realms," I reflected.

By having done just that, I found myself ending my journal entry with the words: "Today I feel hopeful again and better physically. It's a new day, and I will continue with treatment. I am not alone. I never was, and I never will be."

A Hair-ful Life

Like Dominic, I entered this world with a head full of hair. Chalk it up to our Mediterranean roots. We each floated in our amniotic world with luscious black tresses that swayed with the internal rhythms of our safe, secure cocoons. Even our twin daughters, born two months early, made their debut with a complete "do." On the night of their birth, a NICU nurse exclaimed, "They are beautiful! We don't often get to see hair on the heads of our NICU babies!"

When my oncologist first reviewed the primary side effects of the two chemo drugs I'd be given, hair loss was at the top of the list of those guaranteed bodily changes.

"Don't you want to get a wig?" my sister had asked me. I knew I would never be a wig woman. Instead, being a hippie bohemian at heart, it would be scarves and hats. I guess I'm a product of the times when I went to high school—the late sixties and early seventies.

As I organized my closet with comfortable clothes for daily treatment and my new vibrantly colored head accessories, it hit me. "I've never been bald before! Not even at the very beginning of my life. My scalp has never been completely exposed … ever!"

What will it look like? I wondered. In my late teens to early thirties, I had long, waist-length hair. I wore it pasted to my head and secured in a bun or some sort of up-do when I waitressed in my first job. I got quite creative with the twists and knots and braids I designed atop my head. Even when I later worked in an office, I often wore my hair up—secured so I could wear a colorful, stylish hat—one of my signature looks of the eighties. Dominic lovingly referred to my topmost appendage as an egghead because of its apparent shape. *Will I be able to see that egg now for myself? How white will my scalp be? Will my head feel smooth?* I contemplated these questions as I prepared for the inevitable.

I'd taken it in steps, getting myself closer to the ultimate look I'd wear in the months ahead. First came the very short haircut. I knew it would make shaving my head easier—the next step I planned to take. That cut helped me see that I could pull off a very short look. It was even sassy looking and made me feel younger. Who knew? *Maybe I* look *younger too,* I considered.

My hair began falling out around week three of my treatment—not in clumps but just enough to notice lots more hair on my pillow and in the shower. Within a couple of days after noticing that, I could grab the hair at the nape of my neck and pull it out without any effort … or pain. At least not any physical pain. The following day, the hair at the crown of my head released itself into my hand without any resistance.

That morning I pronounced, "It's time!" I knew this day would come, and we were prepared. As Dominic stood behind and above me, I told him I was ready.

In front of our bathroom mirror, we prepared, wrapping towels around my shoulders and over my lap and then placing more towels on the ground to collect my hair as it fell. We would soon discover together just how similar to an egg my head really was.

An egg represents new birth, resurrection, fertility. Soon enough, I would rise from the despair of this experience. A new woman transformed, reborn, and ready to live life fully and with abandon. Yes, an egg held profound meaning for this time in my life and the way I needed to approach it: with ease, grace, and gratitude ... EGG. The words and acronym meant even more than I'd understood previously. I would celebrate my egghead, knowing that with it, new life and rebirth would come.

I smiled at Dominic, and with tears in my eyes, I finally spoke. "Let's do it!"

Smiling back at me, he responded, "Okay."

Today is the beginning. Today is the day I shed the old. Today is the start of the new—of what is to come.

I was ready. The hum of the electric razor sang out—it was time to be set free.

Autopilot

L ooking back at the two months of treatment, much of what I experienced is a blur—there are even gaps. I have no recollection of what occurred at certain points in the process, when it seems I let what was happening carry me along, whether it was the treatment, the side effects, or the support, both seen and unseen. I was not fighting this current—I didn't have the energy to try to paddle upstream. I was not expressing emotion. I had to stay the course and ride the wave without analyzing it or responding to it. I had to allow myself to merge with what was happening to my body, with what was being done to me. I had to surrender. At those times, the entirety of me went into autopilot mode, allowing the "container" I was in to move me along.

At one point, the pain I experienced was so excruciating that it "brought me to." I remember sobbing and crying out to Dominic,

"I can't do this anymore! I just want to die!" I know that scared the hell out of him—it sure scared me to think I could feel this way when, more than anything in the world, I wanted to live. It was as if I'd been on autopilot for a time, and then the pain I was experiencing in my back, belly, mouth, and butt woke me up. It was too much to bear. I didn't know how I could go on.

I remember Dominic comforting me and rubbing my back as he spoke words of encouragement. "You can do this, Donna. You will get through this. I know you will. We will get through this together. You are the strongest person I know." I felt everything but strong at that moment, but I let his words and his stroking soothe me.

That moment of *coming to* reminded me of another time in my life when I'd gone into autopilot mode for a few minutes before I woke up and realized what was happening. That was when fear and desperation came online, and I had to navigate it and stay as present as I could to what was happening and what I needed to do.

Our girls were about four years old, and I had taken them to our community pool for a day of swimming with another friend and her twins, a boy and a girl. My daughters could swim proficiently by then, and they were allowed to go in the deep end. The pool was small, so if they stayed where they could stand up, it didn't give them much room to swim around. My friend's children did not yet know how to swim, and they were at an age when they no longer wanted to wear floaties—it was too babyish.

Initially, my girlfriend insisted they stay where they could touch the bottom, and I instructed my girls to stay with them. That worked for a while, but soon, my daughters wanted to go into the deep end, even being able to get out and jump off the side. They also wanted to use their kickboards in the deep end. At first, I said no. The negotiating continued as my friend's children begged her to let them go into the deep end too. She finally succumbed and told them they could, as long as they held on to the side to move around the edge of the pool. She said they could also use the girls' kickboards as long as they held on tight. Since she felt comfortable with that arrangement, I finally allowed my girls to go into the deep end.

Time passed, and we kept an eye on everyone as she and I continued to chat. As we were talking and I watched the kids in the pool, something caught my eye. For a split second, I turned back to her to respond to what she was saying and just as quickly realized I needed to look back to the pool. Her daughter was floating face down at the center of the deep end with the kickboard a distance away from her. She was not moving. "Oh my god!" I yelled and then screamed out her name. With that, my girlfriend turned around to look. She flew out of her seat, ran to the pool's edge, and jumped in. Just as quickly, she reached her daughter and grabbed her, turning her right side up and lifting her above the water. Sobbing and cradling her in her arms, she repeatedly screamed her name. I could see that her daughter's face was blue. My girlfriend continued to hold her and look at her, all the while screaming her name in an attempt to get her daughter to wake up.

The next thing I remember is realizing I was leaning over her daughter as she lay on the ground at the side of the pool while I attempted to administer CPR. Desperate to get her breathing, I tried the techniques I remembered from my training. With each attempt, nothing happened. I felt fear and panic ramping up, sensing that it was up to me to bring her back to life. *But why isn't it working?* I screamed for someone to call 911 as I continued. Finally, I swept my finger in her mouth and turned her once more on her side. Her gag reflex kicked in, and water rolled out the side of her mouth onto the ground. She choked and sputtered, but she was breathing. Relief swept through me as tears came. "Thank god she is alive!" I said as my body began to shake uncontrollably.

Later that night, when her parents came over to tell us she was okay and had been released from the hospital, I felt immense gratitude. My attempts at CPR hadn't been textbook, and at first, I felt tremendous guilt because it could have cost her life, but the police officer who interviewed me at the scene said that no matter how I'd done it, I saved her. He then smiled with compassion in his eyes and pointed to the big, printed boards on the cabana building. "I hope you never have to do this again, but if you ever need to, have someone read out those instructions to you. They're all there … what to do for a drowning victim. No matter what, though, don't forget: you saved her life."

As Dominic and I talked with her parents, I finally turned to her mom and asked the question that had been going through my head over and over: "So I remember you jumping in the pool, holding her up, and crying out her name, but the next thing I remember is leaning over her on the side of the pool. How did she get there? I don't remember what happened."

"Oh my god," her mother said. "You yelled at me to hand her to you. You told me to do it *now!* I brought her over to you, and you took her from me and laid her down on the side of the pool. Then you started doing CPR. I don't know what I would have done if you hadn't yelled at me to get her to you. I was panicked."

Dominic had told me many times that I go into "fix it" mode whenever there's a crisis or significant problem to address. I immediately get to work trying to find the right solution. He knew how to do that in a cockpit because of his training and experience, but when it came to everyday life dilemmas, he froze. He'd told me in the past that if there ever was a time when I didn't see the possibility of options, that's when he'd panic.

Thankfully, in this near-drowning scenario, that part of me that sets aside all emotion to take over and deal with a crisis did just that. Even once I was aware of what was happening and fear kicked in, I forced myself to stay in control. As a result, a child was saved.

While I went through treatment, that was my *modus operandi*. I went into autopilot at times, when all I could do was go within, when emotions were turned off, when I hung on and rode the perilous waves. At other times, I was aware of what was happening, and I instructed myself to stay in control by trusting the process and the people navigating the ship. Again, keeping my emotions at bay.

On this one occasion, though, as the intense pain seemed to swallow me whole, I found myself scared and desperate. I didn't know how I could hold on as my boat rocked and rolled in the violent storm. No longer contained in the eye of the storm, I was being knocked around, and I didn't think I could survive it. Fortunately, Dominic was able to pick me up and carry me to a place where I could once again ride through this experience. Although he never thought he could do it if I ever lost sight of shore, he found his true north that day and carried us both through to safety.

Hospitalizations

After both chemo weeks, I ended up in the hospital. The first time, I began experiencing extreme abdominal pain on my right side. We made an emergency appointment with my oncologist, and I was wheeled into her office. She immediately ordered a CT scan and sent me next door to the hospital. Initially, she thought it was my appendix. I didn't make a connection to the diverticulitis I'd been hospitalized for in 2008—my one and only experience with diverticulitis. The CT scan confirmed that it had flared up, and my oncologist ordered that I be immediately hospitalized and put on a three-day course of IV antibiotics. Thankfully, the abdominal pain began to subside within the first twenty-four hours.

The second time I was hospitalized, it turned out I'd developed C. diff. After being given the course of heavy antibiotics for the diverticulitis, followed a few weeks later with my second five-day round of chemo, my immune system was shot, which allowed the C. diff to develop and rage. I landed in the hospital for eight days as they worked to get it under control. I wouldn't be allowed to go home until I was fever-free and able to eat soft foods, as well as experience five or fewer bouts of diarrhea per day. When I was admitted, and for a number of days thereafter, I experienced diarrhea in excess of twenty times a day.

The requisite treatment was more antibiotics—a special one that was administered orally in liquid form. The taste was so horrible and repulsive that I asked if there was anything to mask it. A nurse suggested a popsicle chaser, which turned out to be a great solution. As soon as I swallowed the bitter medicine, I began sucking on the orange-flavored popsicle—and because I had to suck on it slowly, it helped eliminate the lingering bitter taste in my mouth.

Juice wasn't an option since it exacerbated my digestive symptoms. My raw butt and the diarrhea, now further complicated by the heavy antibiotics, were excruciating. Every time I had to use the restroom, I dreaded what I knew was coming. Severe abdominal pain and extreme burning as "waste" left my body. I could hardly bring the sensitive-skin baby wipes to my backside. My mouth sores continued to rage—another reason juice was not a viable choice.

Although I was in constant pain throughout my body, in my mouth, and on my backside, I was grateful to be in the hospital where I could be monitored and where the nurses did as much as they could to help, including administering IV fluids to keep me hydrated and IV pain meds when I couldn't tolerate the pain any longer. As much as I wanted to go home, I knew it would be difficult to leave the cocoon of the hospital, where I was tended to around the clock. Not being a demanding person, I tried to manage as much as I could on my own, but when necessary, I could count on my daily and nightly nurses. I knew I was in good hands—caring hands—of people who wanted to see me start to feel better. For that, I was grateful.

Yes, You Were the Right Doctor

With each hospitalization, we had to make decisions about my treatment since it was the treatment that contributed to the illnesses I developed. The protocol for treating anal cancer was specific: two five-day rounds of chemo four weeks apart and a simultaneous six-and-a-half-week course of radiation five days each week. Taking too many breaks in the treatment or ones that went on for too long could reduce the chances of the desired outcome: eliminating the tumor.

The first hospitalization did not interfere with sticking to the chemo schedule. I would be well enough and able to continue with the second round of chemo at the prescribed time. The three-day stay did halt radiation, but my oncologist assured me that the delay would not put the treatment plan in jeopardy. It was the second hospitalization that required considerable thought and discussion about how and when to proceed. By then, I had completed my second round of chemo and was almost through my sixth week of radiation, but I still had about one week of radiation to complete.

In the midst of discussions about how to proceed, which included communication between my primary medical oncologist and my radiation oncologist, the questions on the table included how long we could reasonably wait to restart treatment without risking a good outcome and a clear prognosis moving forward. This was when I knew beyond any doubt that I had chosen well.

I had not considered choosing a different radiation oncologist, but I had spent significant time deciding which of the two medical oncologists I would use. The deciding factors had been my oncologist's compassionate bedside manner, her ability to truly listen, and my sense of her spiritual connection. I knew she was knowledgeable and experienced—as had been the other oncologist—but her demeanor and heartfelt wisdom were part of the unseen that I needed to support me.

With the first hospitalization, her actions were swift and decisive. *Wheel her to imaging to get a CT scan and, based on the results, get her admitted immediately.* She took the same approach with the second hospitalization: *get her admitted immediately and start treatment.* Discharge after the first hospitalization was clear-cut, too—after a three-day course of IV antibiotics, it was time to go home. The second time, however, required not only consultation with the radiation oncologist but also with the infectious disease doctor and the hospitalist. Everyone put their heads together to keep me in long enough to abate the infection yet swift enough to get me back to treatment.

I remember telling my oncologist that I was fine if we had to delay for a couple of weeks. I was still in so much discomfort from the effects of treatment as well as the C. diff coursing through my body that I was looking for a reprieve. I was even willing to stop radiation altogether and not finish the final week of treatment. She smiled at me with genuine compassion. "We need to make sure we get restarted as soon as your body can handle it, but unfortunately, it won't be when you are feeling 100 percent. It will be when the C. diff is under control. We want the best outcome for you so you can go on to live many, many more years ... so we cannot delay unnecessarily."

Her demeanor, facial expressions, and tone of voice spoke volumes. She was sympathetic to my desire to put on the brakes, even to bail from the course altogether, but she had to look at it from a medical perspective to achieve the best possible outcome. I had to trust her, and I did. I also knew she'd walk through the rest of this with me as much as I needed.

After eight days, I went home with the continuation of the liquid antibiotics, baby wipes to address my raw, painful backside, and a mouthwash to soothe the mouth sores that continued to rage. I was still weak and had lost significant weight, but my body had regained enough strength to go home and continue radiation. I'd been in the hospital since May 2 and went home on Friday night, May 9. On Monday, May 12, I resumed my radiation treatments following a quiet and restful Mother's Day weekend when I heard from my daughters and was visited by the one who lived nearby. It was so good to be home and feel everyone's love and support. I would get through the rest of the treatment because I had much to live for.

Although I'd been ready to stop treatment while in the hospital because I wanted relief from so much pain, once we were ready to resume treatment, I wondered if I'd jeopardized the chances of eliminating the cancer. *Had we taken too long of a break in the treatment?* When I talked to my oncologist about my fears before I left the hospital, she reminded me that I'd completed chemo on schedule and had twenty-seven radiation treatments before I was hospitalized. Essentially, I'd been "close to done." She was not in the least bit worried. She felt we were now on course for the home stretch. She also told me that one of her colleagues builds in a break during treatment because the regimen for anal cancer is so hard on the body. I couldn't deny that—my body was definitely suffering internally and externally.

Originally, I'd been scheduled to complete radiation treatment on May 7, 2014. Instead, I completed my thirty-third session on Monday, May 19. After I was done, the radiation staff sent me off with hugs and smiles, as well as a bag containing two chocolate chip cookies and a card signed by everyone in the radiation department. It was graduation day, and I was being sent home with congratulations and cheers for my growing strength and good health ahead.

Ultimately, I also had the port removed and was given that big giant chocolate chip cookie by the medical staff, just as the physician who'd placed my port promised. He wasn't there on the day it was removed, but I thought of him and his beautiful smile and calm demeanor as the port was ushered away.

This had not been a walk in the park by any stretch of the imagination, but I had been supported and cared for throughout these intense months. As we made each tough decision, I had been listened to and considered. My most significant realization during my hospitalizations was how calm and discerning my oncologist had been every step of the way. She never got rattled or became indecisive. Each pause was intentional as she gathered information to decide what would happen next and when. She stayed involved and collaborated with the other doctors, especially throughout my second hospital stay. Through it all, I'd known I was in good hands and never once doubted her ability to make decisions. I never felt the need to question the decisions she came to. For those reasons, even in the midst of a scary and painful time, I was grateful. Because of her deep conviction, I knew I'd make it through. Ultimately, I did.

Limb Alert

E ach time I've been hospitalized since my mastectomy, I've received a bright pink bracelet with the words "Limb Alert" on it. I've hated that bracelet! In the past, it's reminded me that I have another weakness. The lymph nodes that were removed along with my right breast mean I can never have my blood drawn or my blood pressure taken on my right arm. Nurses and techs say it's too risky.

I've never had lymph drainage issues on my right side; I've had no sign of lymphedema in my right arm. There's never been any indication of swelling or discomfort or pain as some women experience after a mastectomy and the removal of lymph nodes. However, medical staff don't want to do anything that might create an issue, which, apparently, blood draws and blood pressure monitoring could create.

The rebellious part of me has wanted to do it, just once. "Let's see if it causes a problem," I've challenged nurses and techs. I honestly don't think it will. But no one is willing to play along. No one is willing to take a chance and risk causing a problem that doesn't currently exist. So, unless I someday get rebellious enough to hide this information from some unknowing tech before they realize I've had a mastectomy, I'll continue to comply. As much as I want to defy protocol and prove to myself and others that I am strong in every way, another part of me says, "Let's be practical. Let's be realistic here. And let's not tempt fate to try and prove a point. Be the compliant patient at least when it comes to this—a minor thing that seems to only bother your ego but has no other consequence."

So far, that voice of reason has won out. I've learned to wear my "limb alert" bracelet quietly. I don't wear it proudly and doubt I ever will. But I am learning once more that ease and grace and gratitude, along with a good dose of humility, can go a long way to keeping me safe and alive and even comfortable.

Tumor's Gifts

I knew I needed to release this tumor, not only on a physical level but also from a spiritual level. I needed to be able to bless and thank it for showing up and showing me what I'd not wanted to look at before. I needed to find humility in and acceptance of the medical process necessary to physically dissipate it. Ultimately, I needed to let this tumor go energetically, even if the work of being with and releasing all that it represented would take many more years.

As I continued to endure the effects of treatment, I could at least begin to look at why it might have shown up in the first place. It wasn't that I'd done anything wrong. It wasn't because I should or shouldn't have acted in certain ways. It simply was time to look deeper within myself and to face my fears around the treatment modalities I'd hoped to never have to embrace. Here I was being given the chance to see both the messages from my tumor and the treatment to transmute all of it into gifts. As hard as it was on some days—especially when I got dehydrated, when the nausea got intolerable and I needed IV infusions to help me, when the mouth sores or a bowel movement brought tears to my eyes, or when the pain in my back from the injections to increase my blood cell supply got excruciating—it wasn't so easy to see those gifts. But I persevered. On most days, I was determined to find my way through.

Before I began treatment, I'd considered where this cancer manifested. In my anus. Close to the exit of my body but still inside it. Connected to the root chakra. Connected to the core foundational aspects of one's life. Connected to my core sense of self, my sense of safety and security. Admittedly, the prior few years had been extremely difficult and culminated in marital separation and both of our daughters moving out at eighteen. The pain and grief and anger and guilt that accompanied those events were intense. Yet, I tried each day to get up and find my way through the darkness, focusing on my work and my hopes for the sale of our family home. I put all my energies into what I could influence and manage while other parts of my life were completely out of control.

By the time the tumor was discovered, Dominic and I had reconciled. We had tried unsuccessfully to sell our family home and were still grieving over the loss of our two daughters from our home, especially one of our daughters, who was now estranged from us. But because he and I were together, I felt stronger and more hopeful. I was also grateful our home hadn't sold—it allowed me to go through treatment and be in a physical place that was familiar and felt safe. So, with the tumor's discovery, I had asked what else its appearance was about.

As I sat in meditation and journaled, I saw all the dark shit I tried to keep hidden, all that I tried to prevent from showing up in the light of day. All that I squeezed in, all that I tried to hold in tight, like trying not to pass gas in public. All that I didn't want others to know about me. Hidden, or so I thought, so that others would only see the version of Donna that had it all together, the strong woman who managed whatever came her way, who coped with the ups and downs and then moved on—all with a poker face and sometimes even a smile. I saw all that I didn't want to let seep out.

Yes, I'd tried to keep it all inside, but it wanted to be released— all the anger, fear, jealousy, grief, shame, lack of self-worth, insecurity, physical disconnection even from touch. All the beliefs that held me back and kept me separate from others, feeling a lack of belonging and an overwhelming sense of loss. All the mistakes, missteps, and pain I'd experienced and caused or contributed to others. All the humiliation that lay in my long-ago past and the guilt of not being a good parent. All the realizations of my part in the demise and near-death of my marriage. All that I had tried to deny. All that I'd tucked away and tried not to express. All that I'd tried not to let others know about me. All of it had been contained in a tumor that was no bigger than a grape. When I thought about its size, it was minuscule, considering all that I worked so hard to contain and keep hidden.

I still needed to release some patterns as well. One was the ongoing cycle of fear I allowed to run me in many different areas of my life. After I completed treatment, it showed up as fear that the cancer wasn't completely gone, especially because of the break in treatment necessitated by my second hospitalization. Once my oncologist assured me that we had not jeopardized a good outcome, I still felt fear come up in those first couple of weeks after I got home. It was easy to hang my fear on that circumstance. Yet, I had to make a choice: I could hang on to fear or let it go. I could see the inner walls of my anus as smooth, or I could still see a residual bump. I could hold on to suffering and disease, both of which I'd just experienced, or I could choose to start living in the light with gratitude, joy, and present-moment bliss. It was up to me.

I tended to hold on to everything, especially grief. Grief was my other go-to pattern of behavior, and it debilitated me at times. I knew grief blocks any possibility of joy and drains my life-force energy, but I couldn't seem to release it. I was certain that I even carried generational and cultural grief on behalf of my Italian-Catholic lineage (or because of my lineage).

In a sense, all that I carried deep within had started to rot from the inside out. It would continue to do so—energetically, if not physically—unless I began to allow for the release of all that I was hiding. If I was going to go on and live, it had to come up and out, and I had to let it go. If I was going to not just try to survive, if I wanted to truly thrive, it had to be acknowledged, embraced, and loved—all of it. The tumor and all that it contained, as well as the treatment that had been required to eradicate it, all had to be released.

Rather than living in the shadows or remaining on the sidelines of life, I could now choose to live my life fully. I truly was being given another chance to thrive—maybe my last chance. After seeing how sick I'd become, now I could grab on to health and vitality and let go of the old patterns, the deep-seated traumas and injuries of the past that could pull me away from what I most desire for myself. After seeing people in the treatment rooms, young and old, who might not live for much longer, I knew how fortunate I was. On the last day of May 2014, I wrote in my journal:

"I cannot squander this gift I've been given. I get to live and live on for a long time to come! I get to *thrive!* I get to experience love and joy and life and compassion and forgiveness (for others, but most of all, for me). I get to travel and work and play and sing and dance. I get to *be!* So today, on this New Moon, I release cancer and disease and illness and sickness. I release sorrow and suffering and pain and drama. I release fear and worry and doubt. I release living halfway.

"Today, I choose life. I choose joy. I choose to thrive and blossom and flourish. I choose to be present, to show up, to be exposed, to be authentic, to be real, to be me. I choose to trust again. I choose to live fully, and I choose to do it now. If not now, when?"

It wasn't yet time to process everything I'd tried to hide. I did not have the strength or ability to do so as I went through treatment and began to recover. But by starting to acknowledge what was there and opening myself to the promise of one day looking at it more deeply and releasing it with gratitude so I could go on and truly live with purpose and intention, I could now move forward.

More Gifts

Initially, the most tangible outward sign of healing and the return of strength to my body was the regrowth of my hair. By the time I was undergoing my final week of radiation, fuzzy stubble had begun to appear on my head. After the incredibly intense treatment my body had been subjected to, just like the beginning signs of growth as a seedling juts forth from the thawed winter ground, tiny "hairlings" began to sprout over my entire bald head. As these saplings appeared, for the first time, I had a visible indication that I would regain my health. I was in awe of my body's ability to begin to heal itself even as I finished up the last of my treatment. And not only was it healing, but those hairlings also signified my body's regenerative abilities. I felt utter reverence for each and every cell in my body that wanted to thrive during its individual life span, despite the bombardment my body underwent.

Because I'd colored my hair since I was forty-one years old (the first time being just a few days before my father's funeral), I had no idea what my natural color would look like. Just as I'd not wanted family or friends whom I hadn't seen in at least two decades to know I was graying back then, I also didn't think I wanted people to realize that, in my late fifties, my hair was no longer completely brown or maybe not brown at all. I'd initially decided to color my hair as soon as it grew in enough to be color-treated. Based on what I'd seen in the past when my roots began to grow out, I suspected that my real, late-fifties color was a drab gray, not a becoming look for anyone. That drab gray hinted at completely washing out my facial features, making me look forever ill.

Boy, was I surprised by the shiny silver that began to pop out, glinting in the sunlight whenever I sat outside! At first, I couldn't believe it. Yet, there it was! Silvery sparkling stubble. Not a hint of the drab I'd expected. Even the radiation techs began to comment on how gorgeous my natural hair color was. They'd both seen my colored hair before I shaved my head, so they seemed as pleasantly surprised as I was at what was sprouting.

That's when new questions entered my mind. *Is it possible that my natural color* will be *so pretty that I won't want to color it anymore? Could I allow myself to show up authentically from the top down? Am I brave enough to let my status as a crone, as a strong, independent Amazon woman, be visible? Will my gray hair make me look and feel old, or will it make me feel more powerful?*

And I began to dream. *Wouldn't it be wonderful not to have to color my hair every six weeks? Wouldn't it be freeing to have a true wash n' wear hairstyle that requires no other maintenance beyond haircuts every four to five weeks?*

Rather than an all-or-nothing decision, though, I decided to take a wait-and-see approach. Let my hair continue to grow back, have it cut and shaped along the way, and decide how long or short to ultimately wear it. In the midst of that process, see how my hair looks and how I feel about wearing it naturally. Let time provide the answers.

As many weeks passed and it was time to go to my hairdresser for a trim, the answer was clear. *Let this gorgeous, silver-and-black hair that is growing in stay. Allow this gift to be with you—to become a part of you.*

Many years earlier, as I saw the gray showing up in my roots, I'd contemplated the process of growing out my natural hair color. I'd discussed it with my hairdresser at the time, and she suggested that if I wanted to do it, we could start to color my hair silver so that as it grew out, the roots could be blended. Finding the right color would be a bit of trial and error, but she thought we could find one that would look beautiful. At that time, I decided I wasn't ready. I wasn't brave enough for such a drastic change.

Cancer gave me the opportunity to make that shift without any other preparation. Here I was *au naturel*—not only an Amazon woman but now also a spunky silver fox.

The final gift I received after I was completely healed were the words spoken by the colorectal surgeon. When I went in for my first post-treatment appointment in the fall, he once again did a digital exam with an anoscope so he could see and feel the area. This was the appointment I'd been most nervous about. Would he find that the tumor was completely gone, or would he say that I needed further treatment, which meant surgery and the loss of my sphincter muscle? As I lay on my side, he spoke the words I'd been hoping to hear: "It's as smooth as a baby's bottom. The area is smooth and flat. This is wonderful! I'll check you again in six months and continue to check you every six months for the next couple of years, but the tumor is gone. Congratulations!"

I cried with gratitude. My health was restored, I was regaining my strength, I now had a head of silvery hair, and the cancer had been removed. I could not have received any greater gifts.

Third Movement

I Never Expected ...

I never expected to get cancer. Who does? I guess nobody ever intends to get sick or find out they have a disease. Why would they? There is just no way to prepare for the eventuality of news like this. The day I was told for the first time that I had cancer was one of the most shocking and excruciatingly painful days of my life. I still see myself sitting down in the chair at the desk in my bedroom as I took the call.

Hearing the pronouncement, "It is cancer," took my breath away, and yet I wasn't completely surprised by this proclamation. From the way the technician had responded to my leading questions and statements on the day of my biopsy, I had a sinking feeling I would find out I did, indeed, have cancer. Until that call came in from the radiologist, however, a part of me held on to hope that my attempt at reading between the lines would turn out to be wrong. For once, I really did want to be proven wrong!

As the radiologist gave me the news, I wrote down notes using the pen and paper Dominic handed me. Somehow, he knew I'd need to record what I was being told because once I hung up, I probably wouldn't remember everything. His instinct turned out to be right—had I not written down what the radiologist said, I would not have been able to explain much of it to him or anyone else.

"Grade 1, least aggressive type, small area approximately 1 cm. in diameter. Stage? Can't determine that until biopsy. Can schedule appointment for second biopsy—sentinel node. Make appointment with a surgeon. Find one. Decide what to do. If no lumpectomy, no biopsy. Can find out grade in surgery. Mastectomy. Call surgeon—make appointment."

After I hung up, we went over and over them. What did it mean? What should I do? Who should I call? Where should we start? "Let's just get it out. The sooner, the better," Dominic said to me. For him, it couldn't be soon enough.

The day I was first diagnosed was a day full of beginnings, some of which I was aware of and others I wouldn't see until much later. I would begin to deal with a disease I had hoped never to have to deal with (although in the back of my mind, I'd always worried that one day I might). I'd need to begin the process of making decisions. Little did I know that this process would also be the beginning of finding my voice and speaking up for myself in significant ways. It was also the beginning of taking inventory of my life—how is it that I ended up at this particular place?—and understanding that if I didn't find out how to love, tend to, and care for myself, I might not make it through this bump in the road.

That day was also rich with endings. First was the ending of being able to check all the "nos" on a doctor's form. It was also the ending of believing that my body was invincible. Even more important, it represented the ending of believing *I am invincible.*

Nothing has or ever will be the same as a result of that phone call on February 14, 2007. As sad as that news was, and as sad as I can still get sometimes about the cost of that diagnosis to me mentally, physically, and emotionally, I know now that I was given a gift on that Valentine's Day: to fall in love with me—to love myself and learn how to nurture and care for me.

My second diagnosis on a second Valentine's Day seven years later was equally shocking. Along with a completely different cancer, it required a completely different treatment. It also demanded that I look at how I'd been treating myself and my life. It's true that I'd become complacent in how I cared for myself. As my family began to fall apart before my eyes, I did everything humanly possible to control the fallout. In the midst of my efforts, I once again lost sight of myself—my health and my self-care needs. I was back in survival mode, and it wasn't always pretty. I'd stopped living as a life thriver.

My second diagnosis and treatment required that I stop trying to take care of everyone else. All I could do was go inward and focus on making it through the treatment so I could go on living. It was a huge lesson in being able to see that the world and my family would go on, with or without me. If I wanted to be a part of life and living, I had to take care of myself first. It was finally time to take in this lesson of self-care and self-love.

Even though I've accepted the gift of self-love, and over time I've taken it in more deeply, I still don't always get it right. On many days, I know I'm not doing a good job of it, but because of the gift I've received to go on living and the opportunity I've been offered to thrive, I can never ever allow myself to go back to sleep. I know that unless I truly love, care, and nurture myself, I cannot be fully alive. And, unless I practice self-care and see myself as worthy of love, I will wither away. That is not an option—and that is not what I declared to the Universe when I knew what lay ahead after my second diagnosis: "I commit to and declare that if I am given the gift of life, I will do my work in the world and share my gifts and talents to the best of my ability until the day of my last breath."

Today, when I get off track, I come back to that commitment and do my best to take care of myself. After all, no matter what has happened in my life, no matter what I've done or not done, I am worthy of love. Each and every being on the planet is, so why would I have ever thought I wasn't? I have been and always will be.

One More Message

Five years after my mother took my sister and me to Italy to meet our relatives, she wanted to return. Turning eighty-five, she sensed this would be her last visit. Everyone who'd been there five years earlier was still living, even one first cousin who was two years older than my mom.

We planned the trip for late September through early October—two weeks in Montecatini, Monterosso (Cinque Terre), and Florence. Plenty of time to see our relatives at the beginning and end of our trip, and to spend time in places we'd never been before—Montecatini and Cinque Terre.

The trip was filled with highs and a few lows. I'd had to bring work along and was struggling to get it done—to find both the time and space to do it. The three of us hadn't traveled together in five years, so we needed to make adjustments and show understanding, along with the ability to let things go as we shared small quarters together. We managed it fairly well, but we definitely had a few intense moments—old patterns and unfinished junk came up. We did our best to navigate it and found our way back to a peaceful vacation.

I didn't bring my writing along as I'd done the previous year when I'd visited Florence with my girlfriend Rosalie. I knew I wouldn't have time to write. Even my journal, which comes with me almost everywhere, sat in my backpack untouched. It was a good exercise in being fully present and taking to memory as much as I could.

When I returned home, the first topics I journaled about were those family patterns that had reared their ugly heads. The toughest part was seeing how I could go right back to them once I had the right partners for those particular dances. "Work in progress, grace and ease," I reminded myself as I finished writing about those key moments, especially as I looked at my part. And yes, I'd definitely had my part in what played out!

Once again, I was reminded that patterns run deep, and not participating in them to some degree can be a huge challenge. It turned out to be so for me. "Progress, not perfection," as they say in the rooms of AA. I most definitely saw the progress in myself. The biggest challenge was allowing others to be who they are. I saw that I still have work to do in that area, especially when it comes to those closest to me. My inability to accept and even appreciate where someone is at any particular moment showed up loud and clear—especially when it came to people I deeply love. I worked hard to allow them to be who they are.

It was a big eye-opener for my self-acceptance, too, showing me once more that self-love and self-compassion continue to seek my attention as I rebuild my heart. As the saying goes, I can't love someone else and have compassion for them and their life if I don't first have that love for myself. It seems these will be themes for a long time to come, maybe even for the rest of my life as I age and continue to change physically.

As I continued to journal, I transitioned to the unexpected gifts I'd received—some that I could even hold in my hands. A rock from the local sea that a shop owner told me to keep when I admired its beauty in her display of jewelry and pottery. Four placemats with four separate stanzas of a poem about lemons written by an Italian poet; when I asked if I could have a clean copy of the paper placemat that had been under my plate, I hadn't realized I only had one of the four individual stanzas.

The biggest gift of all was from the jewelry designer we met in Florence. We had been in her shop earlier in the day when my sister bought a pair of earrings. Before we left, the woman attending to the shop gave us the card for the store because we said we might return to decide on a couple of rings Debbie and I had seen. The address would help us find our way back.

After the three of us lunched at a café nearby, we decided to return to the shop. Federica, the woman who had helped us previously, was helping a couple who were in the process of buying multiple pieces. Another older woman was standing nearby and offered to help Debbie. She explained that they had two separate lines—one of jewelry made with Murano glass and one of jewelry designed with gemstones and pearls. Debbie wanted to see a faceted ruby ring, and I asked if she had more. The woman pulled out a box with many ruby rings, including a ring identical to the one my sister was considering. Debbie also pointed out a ruby that wasn't faceted. It had caught my eye too.

In the process of trying on rings, we learned that the woman helping us was the designer, Gabriella. She had come down to the shop from upstairs to take a break from her design work and some stressful situation she'd been dealing with. She said she loved to meet the people who buy her work and see what goes home with whom. "Pieces always find the right person," she said. At that moment, I was debating between the two rings—the one identical to my sister's, which was a lighter color and faceted, and the one that was smooth and the color of blood.

"If you pick the one like mine, we'll have the same," Debbie said as she looked down at my hands.

Gabriella added, "Listen to your heart. It knows."

I thought about picking from behind someone's back, someone who could be a neutral holder, and then decided to do as Gabriella had instructed: "Listen to your heart." Immediately, I knew. It was the smooth, dark stone. When Gabriella realized which I'd chosen, she smiled. "You picked the right one," she said as she looked at me intently. "That is the ring ... that is you."

We talked longer, especially after she learned that my mother's family originated in Tuscany—in the Lucca area. She spoke English well, having worked for major US department stores in the past.

I gave her my card so we could connect if she ever came to Colorado. That led to questions about my writing. "I help others write their books, but so far, I haven't finished my own." I told her what had happened the year before in Florence and the clear message I'd received about needing to finish my book.

"And I'm the second person in Florence to give you the same message. You need to finish your book."

A meaningless encounter? I don't think so. I believe with all my being that there are no accidents and encounters are never random. There is always significance. From the shop owner we met in Monterosso, who was from Pacific Grove, California, where Dominic and I married and dreamed of living one day, to Gabriella—the messages were for me to take home. The gifts for me were there if I chose to see them … and to receive them.

Write. Finish your book. Live in Italy or Pacific Grove or Hawaii, or even Colorado. Travel. Experience life. Step into your dreams and your vision. In the process, you will be further healed, and your heart will be made whole.

Mosaic heart? Yes. Broken? Not any longer. All the experiences, the many people I've met along the way, and even the ongoing struggles within my family are the mortar to bind the pieces together and create a whole heart.

"Wholehearted living," Brené Brown calls it.

"Yes," I say. I am wholehearted. I will continue to become an ever brighter and bigger version of wholeheartedness—multifaceted and multicolored.

For whatever number of days that lie before me, my mosaic heart will continue to grow and expand, beating to the rhythm of a life founded in love and compassion for all, but first, and most especially, for me.

A New Prosthesis

One and a half years after my anal cancer diagnosis, I went shopping for new bras and a new prosthesis. It was time. My bras had become tight, and my boobs were significantly different in size. Now, more than a year post-treatment, I had gained back my weight, even more than when I'd started. It was time to accept myself where I was—healthy and a little fuller and rounder in size. The healthy part was easy—the thicker me took a little getting used to. But I'd made a promise. Embrace and love myself at whatever age and size I am and however I look.

I stepped into the dressing room with the fitter—a sweet and gentle young woman who asked if I would mind removing my top, then my bra.

"Oh, that's beautiful!" she said with a big smile.

I looked at her, a little confused. "My old bra?" I asked.

"No, your tattoo," she chuckled.

"Oh, of course." I started laughing too. How silly that I thought it was my bra she was admiring. I'd had my tattoo for so long that sometimes I forgot how it would catch someone's attention who'd never seen it before. In a sense, it had become such an integral part of my body that it didn't stand out to me anymore.

"It's beautiful," she said again.

"Thank you," I replied.

"It's wonderful that you had that done," she added.

"Yes, I'm really glad I did," I said as I smiled back at her.

As she left to get bras and a prosthetic for me to try on, I looked at my naked upper body. *My tattoo* is *beautiful,* I thought. *And it is a symbol of who I've become. A woman who is constantly reminded of her inner strength, her inner and outer beauty, and her commitment to ongoing growth and transformation.*

When she returned, I began trying on the items she'd gathered. Every bra she'd selected was perfect, and the prosthesis was just right too. Her first choice of shape and size turned out to match the contour and curvature of my natural breast. *She is good!*

When she left the room again to grab a sports bra, I realized how different this time was. No more intense emotions. No more shame or embarrassment or grief. No more regret or wishing things were different.

I am, I thought. *Just like the lotus on my chest, I am.*

Thinking of my grandmother, I felt gratitude that I could be here shopping for a boob to make my body look balanced. I am one of the lucky women. Two cancers. Two cures. Two opportunities to go on and thrive. Two experiences offered for growth and awareness. And now two perfect boobs! *I am at peace. At this very moment, I am truly at peace.*

I was reminded of the book I'd ghostwritten during the past year. All we have is the present. That's all there is. No focus on the past or how I wish it could have been different; no shame for what's occurred. No worry about the future and what I hope will happen. No fear about the *what ifs*. Today is all there is. At this moment, I have a husband waiting in the reception area for us to go to dinner, a new bra and a new boob to wear, and a knowing that I will handle whatever comes next with ease and grace and gratitude.

Life isn't meant to be easy, but if I am willing, I can respond to life with openness and as much ease and grace and gratitude as I can muster. No matter what comes, being alive and truly living each and every moment is a divine gift. I plan not to waste a second of it.

Suddenly, I knew my grandmother was with me again. Every guard and guardian and mentor was there too. "Embrace life, Donna! Go forth and live in joy and peace. Do your work in the world as you committed to do."

"Yes!" I answered. "I will. I am. Grace and ease. Grace and ease. Ease and grace and gratitude."

Fourth
Movement

Pieces

We are all wounded. We all experience levels of trauma and drama as we grow up. We experience pain. Some of us experience catastrophic, cataclysmic traumas that leave our hearts shattered. The pieces left can be so tiny and slivered that it's almost impossible to put our hearts back together. It may take years, and even decades, of gathering fragments and shards to try to rebuild our hearts. Some hearts never get repaired or rebuilt whole again.

Others of us experience a lifetime of dysfunction filled with daily themes that run through our childhoods and are carried into our adult lives. We may not have faced a significant sequence of traumatic events, but all of those little daily occurrences of blame, shame, ridicule, and hurt can add up to as much post-traumatic woundedness as if we'd endured and suffered horrendous ordeals. Our hearts get broken, maybe not completely shattered, but they are left in pieces all the same. The fear, self-doubt, empti-ness, and sense of inadequacy can keep us from fully engaging with life, from loving and accepting ourselves completely, from experiencing joy, and from being real, authentic, vulnerable, and self-expressive.

This latter group is where I place myself. I come from a family lineage of suffering and fear; we also carry the inability to believe in ourselves or to see ourselves as human beings worthy of love, happiness, and joy. Most importantly, we have carried the inability to believe that our lives have a purpose and are significant. I come from a lineage of shadow walkers—never stepping out completely into the light or allowing ourselves to shine through the darkness. We didn't think we had anything to share. And we thought we *had to* suffer. We've lived with hearts broken into pieces by our life experiences—at our deepest levels, we've carried shame.

Those broken pieces kept me imprisoned—most of the frag-ments gathered together in a pile and left in the corner. I remained there—confined and caged, broken and hurting, never allowing myself to be seen or heard. It's taken more than six decades to re-alize that I, alone, have held the key to unlock this prison door, to release myself and fly free. It's taken over sixty years to understand that I no longer have to live in this dismal, walled-in cage.

These realizations have been painful to embrace. It was much easier to think that others kept me there. It allowed me to blame *them*. I didn't have to take responsibility. Discovering that I held the key meant I also had the power to gather the pieces of my broken heart and cement them back together. Creating a whole heart was and is completely up to me.

It's taken many years of collecting the pieces, even searching for missing chunks—those that hadn't made it into the pile and some that I purposely buried along the way—to begin the process of recreating my heart. It hasn't been necessary to put my heart back together exactly how it was in the beginning. How could I? Healing requires a willingness to look at the pieces and know them, to understand their messages, and to take in how they can serve me and my life today.

Some pieces have been small and unimposing, while others have been quite large. These pieces have always been here, waiting to be found and rediscovered, waiting for the right moment to emerge, usually as a result of my willingness to look deeply into their meanings. They have been patient and unassuming, with an internal knowing that they were never permanently lost—understanding that someday I would be ready to hold and look upon them. Ultimately, they trusted that one day, I would be willing to reconnect with them and integrate the ALL of them into the becoming of me.

No matter how frightened I might be to peer into their reason for being, I've usually been awestruck by what I discover. It is when I begin to explore, search, and allow for the revelation of who I've always been, who I've become as a result of my experiences, and who I truly am that the magic begins. Time, distance, healing, and wisdom help me make sense of what I uncover and excavate. Those elements allow me to shape and mold the pieces I unearth, etching away rough corners and sharp, uneven edges so the fragments can be fitted together into a beautiful mosaic.

As I work with these fragments, both large and small, do I create something completely new, or do I reorder what is already here? I think it's a bit of both. I can create a dream for my future, I can become more than I've ever imagined for myself, knowing that the pieces have always been here. I get to polish and sand them. I get to move them around. I get to break them into smaller bits or reshape them. I get to place them where I want, reordering and refashioning the colors, shapes, and sizes.

Am I done? Not yet. I may never be. The process of rebuilding my heart continues; more is being revealed. I know I have more pieces to look at, especially related to childhood, motherhood, and the lineage of addiction. I tried the hardest to bury these parts far away from the light of day. It's clear that these areas will require tremendous courage to explore. I know I've been preparing for what lies ahead, and the invitation is there for me to unearth and heal these remaining fragments; I've built my heart to this point so I can look further. With each passing day, I am becoming more and more ready to begin.

My mosaic heart did not need to be created with tiles, plates, and mortar, nor did I need to build two of them. My two cancer experiences helped me find more of the pieces that had been hidden long ago. Cancer showed me the pathways to follow as I began to rediscover and create a stronger, more resilient heart. The key that found me in Florence and the tile pieces Rosalie discovered sit on my desk today to remind me that rebuilding my heart may be a lifelong process and the true work to be done is internal. My stories, the one you hold in your hand, and the one yet to be written are my two mosaics made manifest.

There is and has been no right or wrong to this process, no need for perfection. My willingness to find the pieces and bring them together is what I need most, along with my intention to create a whole heart once more so that I can live fully alive—vibrant with color and light. Enough. Complete in who I am and why I am here. Whole and thriving as I was always meant to be.

Panther returned under the full moon
of a warm July night.
You have listened well.
You are stronger than you think.
With each shedding of all
that is not yours,
you are becoming.
With the rebuilding of your heart,
more compassion is growing.
You are healing.
Shine your light into the world.
You are needed.
Your work is not done.
Be well, my child, and thrive.

Acknowledgments

How do I begin to thank the people who have been a part of this fourteen-year journey to the birthing of *Mosaic Heart?* So many people have been companions, teachers, mentors, and guides along the way as I traversed the arduous landscape of cancer while simultaneously navigating my personal relationships, including the one with myself. Named or not, every individual who crossed my path during the past decade and a half has been an integral part of this journey.

Mosaic Heart might never have come to life had it not been for those who encouraged me to keep writing, to not give up on my story, and to share what I was learning about myself and my changing perspectives. Thank you especially to Andrea Costantine-Ransom, who, from the time we began working on books together, told me I needed to finish my story. And to Lisa Shultz, who modeled how to create a writing life in the midst of helping other authors bring out their stories.

I cannot deny the role my deepest thoughts and feelings have played in teaching me to move beyond anger and fear to a place of compassion and love for myself and others. Above all else, I hold immense gratitude to all the unseen that has supported and taught me along the way and has been there uplifting me each and every time I was ready to give up on my story.

Thank you also to Bobby Haas, my incredible editor, who companioned me through the fine-tuning of my manuscript, serving as friend and cheerleader along with being an expert wordsmith. I knew long before my manuscript was completed that Bobby would be the one to help me refine my story. Along with his expert knowledge of writing, he uses his heart, eyes, and ears to bring out the rhythm and flow, as well as to assist writers in painting a lustrous canvas of vibrant, meaningful wordscapes. I am humbled and forever grateful.

Besides a good editor, a writer needs a great proofreader. Jennifer Jas is my go-to gal—she and I have worked on many book projects together. I am so appreciative of how she has my back to ensure that not only is every t crossed and i dotted, but the words strung together are in the best places possible. To open myself to her expertise and reveal my writing to her has only deepened my appreciation for her brilliant skills.

And, although the words are what makes a book a book, the way those words are presented is just as important. I am forever grateful to Melissa McQueen, founder of Creative Reflections, for the art and cover and interior design she created to illuminate my words.

I have also been inspired by the many authors I've worked with to date. Each and every one has helped me see that when the writing muse won't stop whispering in our ears, we need to take action to tell our stories. Listening is not enough. Our stories matter, and we need to allow them to be written.

Last, and most significantly, I must acknowledge my family, especially my husband and my daughters, as well as my closest friends, for the roles they have played in my life to help me become a better human being. Not only are you supporting characters in my story, but you have been and continue to be the supporting foundation for my life. "Thank you" is hardly strong enough to convey the depth of my gratitude.

About the Author

Donna Mazzitelli believes that finding our voices is critical to living authentic lives. As founder of Writing With Donna and Merry Dissonance Press, Donna is an award-winning writing coach, editor, and publisher. She helps writers connect to their unique core voice so they can share messages crafted with heart. Donna's life experiences, which include two cancer diagnoses and significant personal family loss, have helped grow her heart and compassion, as well as her intuition.

Donna recognizes that everyone has stories to tell. The more we share our stories from our hearts—whether fiction or nonfiction—the more our readers will connect with us and be transformed. This is how we heal ourselves and our world.

Donna continues to work on her own writing. To date, she has written and published three children's books: *Warm Toes, The Great Stirring*, and *The Recycling Project. Mosaic Heart: Pieces of an Unfinished Life* is Donna's first memoir. She has begun work on her next memoir, Madonna Blue Heart, which she intends to release in less than a decade!

After fifty years in the San Francisco Bay Area, Donna resides in Castle Rock, Colorado, with her husband, Dominic, and their loving lap dog, Leo. To learn more about Donna, please visit writingwithdonna.com.

Invite Donna to Your Book Club!

As a special gift to readers of *Mosaic Heart,*
Donna would love to visit your book club
either via video conferencing or in person.

Please contact Donna directly to schedule
her appearance at your next book club meeting.
donna@writingwithdonna.com

Stay Connected!

To stay connected, please be sure to find Donna online at:
Facebook: donna.mazzitelli
LinkedIn: donnamazzitelli
Instagram: donna_mazzitelli
Twitter: @wordheartiste

You can also visit her website: DonnaMazzitelli.com
or drop her a line at donna@writingwithdonna.com.
She would love to hear from you!

And one last favor ...
If you have been touched by *Mosaic Heart*, please be sure to visit
her Goodreads and Amazon book pages and leave a review.
Thank you!

About the Press

Merry Dissonance Press is a hybrid indie publisher/book producer of works of transformation, inspiration, exploration, and illumination. MDP takes a holistic approach to bring books into the world that make a little noise and create dissonance within the whole so ALL can be resolved to produce beautiful harmonies.

Merry Dissonance Press works with its authors every step of the way to craft the finest books and help promote them. Dedicated to publishing award-winning books, we strive to support talented writers and assist them to discover, claim, and refine their distinct voices. Merry Dissonance Press is the place where collaboration and facilitation of our shared human experiences join together to make a difference in our world.

For more information, visit merrydissonancepress.com.